TRUMP MUST WIN

TEISHA POWELL, ESQ.

DEDICATION

I dedicate this book to my children, Madelyn Beverly Knudsen and Johnathan Denton Knudsen and to my amazing sisters, Petergay DeSouza and Bethoyia Powell and to my amazing family and friends, whom I do not even need to name because they know who they are. Most importantly, I dedicate this book to God—the giver of life and hope. I also dedicate this book to all the Americans who love America. You need to understand that President Donald J. Trump is the only option for America come November 2020 and I have written this book to make you aware of the same. My only purpose is to help President Donald J. Trump get re-elected to office come November 2020. Please go out in Drove and go and Help us re-elect the Greatest President of the United States. And the Greatest President of the United States who must be re-elected to make things right for us is none other than the President of the United States, Donald J. Trump. God bless America. and God Bless the President of the United States, Donald J. Trump.

Introduction

Hi, I am Teisha Powell. I am a mother of two five-year-old twins. I am a lawyer in the State of Florida and I have had the privilege of working on national election campaigns in the past before I became a mother. I wish I could be out with all my friends and all those wonderful men and women to campaign in November 2020, but with a full-time career in Law and a full-time role as a mother, this is my contribution to the election cycle. If more conservatives take a stand and do what they can, I think we can get more conservative people into the political arena. I am writing you this guide, which is merely 134 pages, to quickly educate you on why you must vote for President Donald J. Trump and the Republican party come November 2020. I feel my message to you is so urgent that I had to write something quick to get out before the election day in 2020.

What I am doing is offering you simple reasons why President Donald Trump should be re-elected in 2020. This guide is just to give every voting American an opportunity to see President Trump and the strength that he has brought to this country. I believe that every American and their families should live in a great country, and after going over the facts with me in this guide, I think you will also agree that President Donald J Trump is the best bet for America to go forward. Ladies and gentlemen, for a very long time, most conservatives and Christians, such as myself, have been pushed off the main media platforms because the Liberal media wanted to hide the faces of young professional blacks like myself, who understand very well that President Trump is not only for the whites but also for the blacks. President Trump is for Americans! And it is time we get the votes and the message out there. So read along and remember come 2020, Vote for President Donald J. Trump. After reading this guide, it is my desire that you will understand more about what makes a great leader, what your future will be like with Trump in office for another 4 years come 2020, the job growth of America, and how to strengthen the American families. I am not perfect; I am just a Christian lawyer and a mother who happens to want more for myself and this country. I think you are just like me. You probably are a mother or a father, have a job or career, and have a child or children. I am sure that you too want a better future for yourself and your children. I haven't met anyone who said: "Oh, I hope to have a horrible future." We all want good, and we must do what it takes to accept good, which means you might have to vote for a President who is direct but that is okay. It is better to have someone in the office like Trump who is truthful than have someone like Sanders or Biden who are untruthful. You know Sanders, Biden, Warren, and the other Democrats are dishonest people because they are making money hand over fist after leaving the public sector. Show me where you get your money from and I will tell you who you are. Actions speak louder than words! If Biden, Sanders, and Warren really gave a crap about the American people, they would not have been hogging the platform and getting paid millions of dollars per year by lobbyist and Wall Street for their speeches. These politicians like Biden, Warren, and Sanders have choices; they could have easily said no to a corrupt government system, but instead, they are like the politicians of the past who line their pockets with cash in exchange for trash for us—the Americans.

Chapter 1

Don't Take a Chance, Trump is your Best Pick for 2020

In today's election cycle, do not take a chance. We know that President Trump is strong on the borders. Would you want criminals coming into your country? Would you like to be rapped or killed by terrorists? I would think your answer is no, in which case I would advise you to not vote for the Democrats in this election cycle. Let's face it; the Democrats said anyone who wants to come to America should come. The Democrats do not believe in screening anyone, because after all if someone tells you that they are not a terrorist, you must just believe them. The Democrats, all the ones running in this election cycle, would love to propose open borders where anyone who wants to enter America should just come. However, President Trump doesn't buy this. President Trump is much smarter than all those Democrats who are running for the office combined. Trump wants to screen the people who come to our country, so we do not harbor terrorists in America. Trump wants to vet the people who come to this country so that we can eliminate the "bad dudes." What is wrong with eliminating bad people from entering a good country? I do not see what the fuss is all about. After all, we close our homes every night to keep bad people from entering into our homes and stealing our belongings, so why should it be any different at the borders? Do yourself a favor and just vote to re-elect President Trump come November 2020. Do not take a chance with the other "so-called politicians." You never leave sure for unsure. Have you ever left a job for no job? I hope your answer is no. Usually, if you are quitting your job, you have something else lined up; it could either be a better job opportunity or you could have found love and had to relocate and hence change your job. Well, think of President Trump in the same way. Trump is the best man to lead this country for the next 4 years. Why go for an unpredictable Democrat who is even unsure on where he or she stands with the voters? It is madness! Keep President Donald J Trump in office and watch this country flourish. Watch as your bank balance increases. Watch as the home equities in your home go higher. Watch as you can cherry-pick a job from the job market. Watch as you can get better health insurance. Watch as the size of the government shrinks. Watch as President Trump balances that big fat ugly American budget. In this way, our children and grandchildren will never inherit a ton of debt from this country. Ladies and gentlemen, this is not a sales picture but the truth. The Bible tells us, "We shall know the Truth and the Truth will set us Free." John 8:32 NIV I am here to tell you that Trump is for us today, Trump is for America tomorrow, and Trump is for America forevermore. So go in droves, get your friends, your neighbors, crap even get your enemies, and get to the voting booths in November 2020 and send a message to Washington D.C. that we are going to keep President Donald J. Trump in the White House. God bless America. God bless the President of the United States, Donald J. Trump.

PRESIDENT TRUMP IS STRONG ON JOBS.

Look at the current job market, whoever wants a job is working. Isn't that good? President Trump is also strong on health care. President Trump had to gut Obamacare as it was a disaster. Obamacare would never have worked out. The government drove out the private sector in health care, which caused a great crash for us in terms of pricing for health care. I know Sanders said that health care is a right and not an option and I agree with Sanders, but the government has no authority or power to handle health care as health care in America is a private sector. The government didn't create health care and the government cannot mandate it. We are not Europe. Most Americans are fascinated by the health care in countries such as Norway or Canada, but have you spoken to people from those countries before? They are paying a pretty penny for their health care. The British people pay around 40% in taxes for health care. Imagine you make 500 per week and 40% of that is paid to health care, which is in addition to the other taxes you have to pay. You are looking at a weekly cheque of around 200 per week. Can you imagine forking over $200.00 per week on a $500.00 per week paycheck for health care? Then, to add insult to injury, most people who signed up for Obamacare were unhealthy and the healthy Americans took the penalty, so this was never going to work. Obamacare needed even healthy people to sign up for health insurance. Now when I was 19 years old going to college, I didn't have a dime to my name. I would go without health insurance because I knew at 19 years old, my chances of getting sick were slim to none. Don't you think other poor young people think the way I do? Yes, of course, they do. This is the problem with the big government. The thinking of the big government cannot be in line with the local people. If President Obama and the Democratic party were thinking clearly and if they were having a relationship with the voters, they would have found out that young poor healthy people do not invest in health care. If you are healthy and poor, why would you buy health insurance? Health insurance is for sick people. Have you read the Bible? Jesus was constantly surrounded by unhealthy people who wanted to get healed (NKV Matthew 8). Jesus had to mention to people, including his disciples, that healthy people do not need a physician. Now, do you think President Obama and the Democratic party were thinking clearly when they started Obamacare? No! They were hoping Obamacare would take a life of its own. It didn't and couldn't, and President Trump did the right thing by gutting Obamacare. We need another four years with President Donald J. Trump in the office to figure out the health care system; Rome wasn't built in a day. I am confident that Trump and the Republican party will come up with a better replacement but we won't know until we re-elect Trump. If you vote for Sanders, Biden, or Warren or any of those other career politicians who are running for President of the United States, they will for sure get us back to Obamacare and stick it down our throats. They know darn well that Obamacare won't work but the Democrats are just hoping to grow the government into a private sector. That way, the Democrats can always have jobs as career politicians. This will for sure kill all the jobs in America and will stifle all the creativity of entrepreneurs who create jobs. Do not vote for the Democrats because they have a lot of dark negative energy that can kill America's dream. I know this as I walked with the politicians on a daily basis. I can tell you the vibes I get when I go to a Democratic event; it is horrible. You feel hopeless. You feel poor. You feel let down. Everyone there just talks about how to create more free money from the government, but no one wants to work. They dream of an America where no one works and money gets printed and comes to our home. Then, food will be rational and very soon they will tell us how many kids to have, where to live, who to date, where to drive, what to drive, what clothes to wear, and so on. This is how tyrants start; they start by offering us free stuff. Think about it. Are you related by blood to Warren, Biden, or any of the politicians running on the Democratic ticket for the President of the United States? The answer is probably no. So, why would a lawyer turned politician have a vested interest in giving you free money? The answer is simple—politicians want to hold on to their power forever and ever. Power is an addiction, which may be even worse than morphine.

In order for the politician to stay in office for the rest of his adult life, he must convince the voter not to work and that everything will be handed down to him/her. The voter, in exchange, might bite that bait. The politician then reigns over the voter for the rest of the voter's life. If we are given free money, we would develop an addiction to laziness. Yes, laziness is sadly an addiction. It is also a sin not to work. If you read the Bible, in the book of Genesis the Lord said by the sweat of our brow, we shall eat bread. To do anything in contrary to that, like live off the land in America for free is a blatant sin. This is why Christians must be a part of the political process. The Democrats will let anything happen. We cannot marry our dogs. We cannot stop working so we can get a handout. We cannot worship whoever we want. We cannot hate people because they are from a different religion. Everything isn't always right. We need to take a stand for truth and righteousness. We must stand up for what is right and what is true. The only truth is found in the Bible and we as Christians must educate other voters on the truth, even if those voters aren't saved. Once the government grows, the people shrink. In order for the government to control our lives, they must first destroy our lives. The Democrats understand that fully well. Do not let them do it. Read your Bible and you will see it is not biblical to be lazy. Nowhere in the Bible does it say that the government should take care of healthy people who have able bodies to work a job. The Bible said if you are poor, then the church needs to handle that (NKV Luke 14:13). The Bible doesn't say not to work and let the government take care of you, instead, the Bible says by the sweat of your brow you should eat Bread (NJV Genesis 3: 9). God is not a man where he would lie (NKV Numbers 23:19). If God wants us to live off the government, he would have written it in the Bible. God would also not have sent us on the earth with talent and gifts. Do you know that work is a way to serve others? When I am a lawyer, I do get paid, but I am serving other people. My clients hire me or even fire me and I am accountable to my clients. That is being in service. Likewise, if you are an Uber driver, you are getting a cheque but you are serving others by driving them to places. Likewise, if you are a landlord, you are serving your tenants. Work is thus a service, and this is the reason why God wants us to do it. It is about being connected to people and showing them love when you get a chance. Now I don't expect you to just witness to everyone you meet at work. But you can smile while you work. If you are having a bad day, you can just wipe it off your back. With the government replacing work with stay home and do nothing, we will not be able to utilize our God-given talent. We probably would also get depressed because there would be nothing to challenge us? I mean every month you will get a cheque from the government without doing anything? Why not just sleep in every day and do nothing? Do you see how unrealistic free is? It is so unrealistic that we should quickly turn the television off when the next Democrats start promising anything for free. It is dry baloney with no bread added to it.

President Trump is the strongest leader running in this election cycle. So why kill the momentum if we have a leader like Trump who can take us in the right direction? I got to say, this is almost like a trick question. I am wondering why so many Democrats are running for the President of the United States when we already have a great President who will be a good candidate for the next 4 years? Would you trade-in your car for an old beat up one? You wouldn't right? This is similar. The Democratic party is asking us to trade in our beloved President for some wanna be politician who can barely figure out if global warming is a hoax. Come on even my five-year-old kids can see through those Democrats. Ignore all those Democrats who are running for the President of the United States in 2020. Do not go to Sanders, Biden, Warren, or any of other Democrats' rallies because you will just be wasting your time. Do not watch the stupid debates of Sanders, Biden, Warren, or any of those silly Democrats running for the President of the United States because you will just be wasting your precious energy. Biden, Sanders, Warren, and the remaining Democrats running for office are just a bunch of confused people who would love to sell books or get air time with CNN. That is what the Democratic party looks like to me. These Democrats are not real; they are full of crap. I mean, Sanders, Warren, and Biden all had their shot at changing the world in their senate seat, but none of them did anything. What makes you think that they will do even more in the highest office? Isn't it obvious they won't? Sanders I heard has become so rich that he cannot even get his message straight. Likewise, Biden will have a problem explaining to the American people how he made millions of dollars after leaving the White House. Where did all that money come from? Which lobbyist did Biden have to sell out to in order to rack in that kind of cash? At least, with Trump, I can see his building and I understand that he is renting properties out to make a living. That would be what any normal hard-working person would do. A crook will just sell his influence to a lobbyist, after all, that is some easy money right there. I know you as a voter are seeing what I can see as well. We both live in America and we are both reading the same paper or watching the same news. However, what I am telling you is not news; I am just showing you that we have a better President than any other options the Democrats are offering us, so why should we settle when we can get another four years of President Donald J. Trump.

President Trump can protect the interest of blacks and all Americans around the world, which is why so many blacks like myself and a lot of black pastors in the American community are backing Trump. We can see that there is a wave of movement for blacks and Trump is for the blacks; Trump is for all Americans. So we better jump on Trump's train or we, as blacks, are going to be left behind for another four years. Do not be fooled by the Democrats; they have nothing to give to the blacks. The Democrats cannot even give the blacks a decent sound bite, yet they promise a better future. I think we as blacks have already put our hats far too long behind the Democratic train ride, and now the Democrats are a train wreck and no sensible black person should ever try to get the Democrats give us anything. We have gotten this far and we now also have Trump on our side (as blacks, it is time for us to get behind the Trump train and vote for President Trump).

We as people need to think beyond the sound bites that will come from the Liberal media. I feel by writing a book this simple, we can get it into the hands of the voters and together we can change this world and we can make America great again for the future generations. If you are like me who loves your family and wants the best for them, I am sure you would want your children and grandchildren to live in a great country and world. No one wishes for their children or grandchildren to be ridden with debt, stress, and evil; everyone hopes the best life for their children and grandchildren. And if this is the case, why would you want to take a chance and destroy their future with a Liberal President in the office such as Biden who Betrayed us by lining his pocket with wall street money, Sanders who is too stupid to lead, or Warren, the wicked one who wants our kids to live off the plantation for free, while her Kids get the top jobs. or any of the others who are running on the Democratic ticket?

Chapter 2

Trump Now, Trump Today, Trump for 2020

Americans, we have a great President! This is something you already know. Our stock market is at an all-time high. The real estate market is booming again and jobs are coming back home. When we have momentum like this with a good sitting President, why would you want to change the tide? We as Americans would be foolish to go and vote for the Democrats, because the last time when President Obama was in office, we as blacks and we as Americans got nothing from it! Absolutely nothing!.

Trump's is in love with his Family

Why did I call this chapter Trump Now, Trump Today and Trump forever or Trump 2020?

Well, Trump represents a lot of glory for America. Let's look at the glory of America and what President Trump stands for. When I was a little girl growing up, I always watched television shows or segments on Donald J. Trump. Let's face it, you might have as well. Trump inspires family every single day. Trump, his family, his lifestyle, and his personality are breathtaking. What makes Trump so fascinating? It's simple. Trump believes in Family as you can see. He might have been married three times, but he was always with his wife, which tells me that family is important to him. He always has his children next to him. If you have children, wouldn't you always want them to be next to you? I understand most of us do not have the luxury to do so because we are not independently wealthy to hire our kids in our jobs. But let us say that we own a business and our kids were capable of working in the business, isn't that what we would want as well? Now, would we think Trump would be a great person if he didn't get along with his kids and didn't have a wife? No, in that case, we would think Trump is strange. The family tells a lot about people. You show me a man with a big family. I will show you a man with a big heart. Family is important. It is the essential of being a person. I find that if someone has strong ties with his/her family, that person tends to have a warm, caring heart. I know your family means the world to you because if they didn't, you wouldn't be pursuing love most of your life. So come on, Trump stands for family and every American stands for family, which alone is a reason enough to vote for Trump. Trump loves his family and demonstrates that family is important to him. If Trump can put his family first, then which American wouldn't want a President who looks after his family with love? Come on. Family is everything and Trump demonstrates that time and time again. We will forever as Americans vote for a President who has strong family ties because we would be able to relate to the President. That President would understand what it is like to have a child go to bed with no food in his/her mouth and because President Trump would feel the same about his kids. So no questions asked, Trump is a good President for America.

PRESIDENT TRUMP'S LIFESTYLE AND CAREER

Let's dive into Trump's lifestyle and career. America is seen by the world as a very rich country. I know you do not feel rich in America because you only have one or two cars in your driveway. But my pastor just told me something. Do you know that if you have two cars in your driveway, you are among the 7% of the world's richest people? That is right. Not many people in the world have two cars in their driveway. I do not know about you, but I am yet to meet an American who doesn't own a car other than because they have a DUI, they cannot drive, or they do not want one because they chose to move to cities where it is not cost-effective to have one. It is not like that in other parts of the world. In places such as Jamaica, owning a car is steep. But as Americans, we do not see it. We just complain about how bad things are and how poor we feel. But I dare you to travel overseas to a poor country and then write or email me to tell me how bad we have things in America. I think your tune will change really quick. You see, when you go overseas and you tell people you are from America, they will automatically assume your life is much easier than theirs; and they are kind of right. When was the last time, someone in America criticized their government and was lead to jail for doing so? Never! This is America for you. Count your blessings! America is a great country. Yes, we can do better, but we are still the greatest country in the entire world and President Trump understands that. I know President Trump inherited money from his father; everyone knows that, but you know what, he didn't squander it. Trump made something of his life and he didn't leave America. Think about that. He stayed in America and made a name for himself because Trump believed in America. When the recession hit, Trump stayed in America and he kept making money. He believed so much in this country that he gave us his own career to become a public servant. Now, if that isn't a quality in a President you can get excited over, I do not know what else to tell you. President Trump is a symbol of what American people crave—success, hard work, family man and sacrifices. Now success is measured in different terms for different people. Some people believe that success is owning a business, others believe success is going to college and graduating or even getting that job promotion. Whatever you envision success to be, consider success to be President Donald J. Trump. This is another reason to vote for Trump. Everyone wants to back a successful person. Ladies and gentlemen of America, there is no other option or successful candidate to back in the President Election of 2020 aside from President Donald J. Trump. So do yourself a favor and in November 2020, vote to re-elect President Donald J. Trump back to the office. That way we can all experience success in our families, in our future, and in our careers. I hope that success is important to you. It doesn't matter how you measure it, but I hope you want to have more than you do today. Why take a chance with those other wheel dealing career politicians when you could have the best person who is already in office to stay in office? And this is why I write this book ladies and gentlemen. I wanted to make sure I can be part of the solution and not the problem. I wanted to educate you in a short period of time on why it is so important to vote for President Donald J. Trump. I feel our very life and our very future depends upon it. Do not let the Liberal media and those career Democratic politicians lead you astray. Nothing good can come from voting for a Democrat in any election. It is the same old same stupid thinking. These career politicians sell you a nickel and covert it to a penny, and then they tell you the penny is worth more than the nickel. Do not fall for it and instead vote for President Donald J Trump come November 2020. Why would you choose to ruin a good thing for all of us? You have families just like me. You want food on your table just like me. And we know the man who can make this happen—ladies and gentlemen, it is President Donald J. Trump.

Trump symbolizes bravery. Another reason why Trump should be re-elected is the symbol President Trump gives to the overseas world. I am now in England while I am writing this book, and when I tell people I am from America, they usually dive into the election era. Most of these people acknowledge that we have a strong and brave President. I have been blessed to travel perhaps once a year overseas for the last 10 years of my life (or even more). So I went overseas when President Obama was in office and while President Trump was in office. I can tell you that the respect I received when Trump was in office was much more than when President Obama was in office. I can tell you that walking around in London, U.K., I feel like I have won the lotto. I can just feel the energy from people when I tell them I am from America. It is amazing to know that President Trump has branded the Americans overseas as brave, giants, and fighters. Why would you want to change a good thing? Go ahead ladies and gentlemen, and do what is right for yourself. Do what is right for your country. Go ahead ladies and gentlemen and vote to re-elect President Donald J. Trump in November 2020.

PRESIDENT TRUMP HAS OPENED OUR EYES TO THE TRUTH

So President Trump has opened our eyes to a lot of facts we already knew but were afraid to accept. Let's talk for instance about China. You do not need rocket science to know that China is cheating its way into being a world leader. And what have the past Presidents of America done about it? Nothing! President Obama was so afraid of the Chinese that he would never call the Chinese out on their illegal trade. But President Trump is no puppet; as soon as President Trump got into office, he went right after China. Now, nothing might come of it, but it is good to bring attention to a cause. Ladies and gentlemen, do you think it is fair for China to steal our jobs? Don't you have kids and grandchildren living in the United States who could use a job? I have two kids and I want them to get a job when they become of age, so should we as Americans just watch all the jobs being sent to China and do nothing about it? Would you allow your enemy to come to your house and steal from you and not do anything? You would not! So why is it okay for China to be stealing from us? It is not!! People will take advantage of you if you let them, and this is the same way countries think too. This is why President Trump said no to China. I know it is tough and we do not understand everything, but the Chinese need to play fair. I do not think anyone has a problem with China becoming a World Leader, but you should not cheat your way into becoming one. And that is why President Trump is trying to expose China. China is unfair in everything it does, and if President Trump doesn't stand up for America, it would just be a matter of time before America would be China's lunch. We cannot sit back and let the Chinese steal us blindly and this is why we need a strong President like Donald J. Trump. We need a strong leader who isn't afraid of any world leader no matter how large that world leader's platform is. China needs someone to stand up to the unfair trade wars and the cheating it has been shaking down on the Americans. And ladies and gentlemen of America, President Donald J. Trump is the reason you should go and vote for his re-election come November 2020 because he has shown us that he is no chicken in dealing with big cheating governments such as China.

PRESIDENT TRUMP LOVES AMERICA

This is obvious, but let me point it out to you. President Trump is a very wealthy man and has billions of dollars. Do you think President Trump needs to work for us, the American people? Not really. You see when you are a billionaire, you are high up on the food chain (after all, we are all animals having a spiritual experience, but that's another story). Mr. Trump hires people for a living, and this might be the first time he has ever been hired. The American people hired him. Do you think a billionaire needs to be President? Not really. A rich person doesn't need anything from us, but we need everything from them. So let us just figure out why a billionaire would become a President?

It cannot be for money because the pay is $400,000. It has to be because he loves the country so much. In fact, there are times when I feel like running for office. I am sure sometimes, you see how things are bad out there, people are evil to each other, and the world is on its way to hell, and we feel the need to do something about it. This is the passion that is required to run for office. Trust me, I have looked into running for a local seat and I just do not have the courage or the salary to do it. Thank God President Trump is super wealthy so he cannot be bought out. This is a good thing for us. And thank God President Trump felt a call to make a change in today's country. We should be happy. We should welcome wealthy people to run for office. Isn't it better for a wealthy person to run for office? Someone who has already made their money in the private sector? That way when that person comes to serve, he will not be motivated by the greed of Washington D.C. I am not a prophet but I am convinced that both Senator Bernie Sanders and Senator Joe Biden will have a hard time explaining to the American voters how they ended up making millions of dollars per year after they held public office? Could it be that both Sanders and Biden sold out to lobbying companies who pay millions per year to do a private speech in exchange for some type of benefit? This is why I am voting for President Trump. It is obvious to me that President Trump loves his country too much to sell out like the career politicians. Let's face it, all the other politicians couldn't make a decent living in the private sector, so they went on to public sector, to use the American people to leverage and brand their names. Then, they (Biden and Obama), for instance, go and make millions when they leave office because now they are really sold out. I am no longer buying that game. My job now is to expose these politicians to you and educate you on why you need the lesser of the two evils. Trump is not perfect by anyone's imagination, but Trump is the best person to lead the American people. End of Story. Go out and vote for a man who loves his country so much that he was willing to give up his own empire (Trump Enterprise) in exchange for becoming the President of the United States. Go out and vote for President Donald J. Trump.

Chapter 3

THE TRUTH SHALL SET YOU FREE.

This chapter is way too easy to write because it is all true. I do not need to make anything up to get this point to you. Please read on to see what I am talking about. I am not able to reach the older black generation because I feel that people like Reverend Al Sharpton and Jesse Jackson have found a way to poison the minds of the elderly black into thinking that the Republican party is for the white man. As a 43-year-old black woman living in America, I can tell you that the Republican party is for everyone. The Republican party is not only for the white men; it is for all men. And this is why blacks need to ponder on why they would want the Democrats when President Trump has a better future for all Americans. I am talking now to the young black voter who is probably in college or you for sure who is under the age of 50. What is in the Democrat's party for you? Absolutely nothing! Most young blacks that I have the privilege of talking to or meeting with on a daily basis, don't really live in the world we once lived in. There are so many opportunities today for young blacks. Yes, there are! I am a lawyer in America making a living and my clients who come to me are diverse. I remember when I was 19 I was told I am black but today, it no longer matters. We are all now so free, and this is why more blacks need to jump ship and come follow me. President Trump is a better choice for the blacks. Here is a sad reality for you all. Most of the abortions clinics in America are in the black areas. Do you know why? It was designed to kill blacks off. Now, you think about that. If you are black, you are probably conservative by nature. I mean, I am black. We all go to church as black people. Maybe the younger blacks do not go, but you know what, the younger blacks are way too familiar with family members who attend church on a regular basis. We believe in Jesus Christ as blacks and we understand that a child is not a fetus, rather a fetus is an unborn child. How can we vote for the Democrats when their platform is to kill black babies? Really. We know the Word of God says killing another person is a sin and abortion should be a crime. It is a crime in other First World Countries such as Ireland and Italy. Why can't abortion be a crime here in America? Do you know how many black babies lives would we save? Where do black lives matter in these debates? Why are people worried about a white cop taking the life of a black boy, but do not protest when white men take the lives of black babies through abortion? Why do we pick one wrong doer to parade but we close our eyes and pretend to the world that the other wrongdoings do not exist? Abortion is wrong; but, of course, in America, we like to pretend that abortion is right and we parade our arrogance around killing babies like it is just some simple medical procedure. One of the main reasons I think abortion is wrong is because it kills so many blacks, which is not a crime according to the government. I understand the way the government thinks. It took me a while to understand this reality. I do not really like writing political books because things tend to be very dark in the political world. There is a lot of negativity in this political space but when I accepted Jesus Christ in my heart, God explained to me why I feel this way in this political space. It is because when you attend church and your pastor tells you killing a child is a crime, you know in your heart you can no longer sit back in this country called America and not spread the news. Ladies and gentlemen, if you are reading this book, I need you to also read the Bible. You really need to see that the Republican agenda helps the black agenda—it helps the Christian agenda. You need to see that the Republican agenda is the only agenda that can save this country. So go out and vote for the Republicans in 2020 and re-elect perhaps the greatest President of the United States, Donald J. Trump.

Chapter 4

HOW ABOUT PEACE IN THE MIDDLE EAST

Do you love wars and rumors of wars? How can you sit still when our nation is on alert about what is going on in the Middle East. Just think Iran. Can you really trust another person in office aside from President Trump? This is a serious time. There is no opportunity for us to feel good about what a candidate likes to say. We need action, as actions speak much louder than words. If it isn't broken, do not fix it. The country is going in the right direction and we have President Trump to thank for that. Since the country is moving in the best direction, we must keep President Trump in the office. If you do not feel that President Trump deserves to be in the office, then think clearly about the Middle East. This will for sure change the way you think. The Middle East is big shit; I do not like to curse, but I do have a 5 year old son living with me. Do you think I want another war? Do you think I want a country where my kids will not grow up well? Do you think I want to be in a country where Iran can beat us at any war? I do not want that whimsy country, nor do you.

It is time for us to be serious about what is happening in the Middle East because most of what happens in the Middle East affects us here in America. I am not only a lawyer and an advocate but I am also a Christian, and most of us in America are Christians too. If you read the Bible, it is obvious that the only side America needs to take is taking a stand for Israel. Why would America take a stand for Israel? It is simple. The President business is Christian business. The President Business is God's business (hence, we need to fight for Israel). The President business is our business; if you believe in God, then you want what Israel wants. We are not left with much choices than to back Israel. The Bible said that Jerusalem is the capital of Israel and there is nothing much we can do about it. This is why it is good to have President Trump into office, who wants to do what is right for Israel. I am not the type of person to speculate, even though being a lawyer for most of my life has turned me into a storyteller. But I can just imagine, it takes comfort for the Jewish people of America to know that President Trump's daughter, Ivanka Trump and her husband Jared Kushner are Jewish. According to a web page on the Internet named www.haaretz.com, Mr. Kushner had met with top Christian leaders to assure these Christian leaders that President Trump is for Israel. Now, you might be wondering, why is Israel so important, and the answer has nothing to do with mortal thinking. I am a lawyer and I got to say lawyers are wise, but this is not something that I got from Law school. This is something I got from attending the church and reading my Bible. You see the beginning and the end of this world has everything to do with Israel. I want you to picture this. There is a God and we are his puppets. God told us through the Bible that Israel is important to us. There is a sitting President of the United States who also believes that Israel is important to America. Do you think these things are a coincidence? Think again. How could a Bible that was written 2000 years ago predict with such accuracy the moves of a standing President of the United States? The United States is the most powerful country in the world and we have the tools available with us to start any world war and to end mankind. We need to stand with Israel if we want to continue to prosper in this country. I have never seen a person succeed who wasn't a Jewish descendant or did something good for the Jewish people. You know I am blessed today because I am in a heavy Jewish profession. I am a black lawyer, but I am blessed because the Lord has blessed the Jews, and I am just getting a ripple effect blessing because I am a Gentile standing next to the Jewish nation. If you want money in your pocket, then vote for President Trump—it is plain and simple. Whatever is good for Israel, is good for America. We will never and can never turn our backs on the Jewish people. Israel is our Christian motherland, and as Americans, we need to adopt Israel like our own. Only vote for Presidents who will back Israel and the only President candidate in this election cycle who will do right for Israel is President Donald J. Trump. If you as an American seek truth, hope, freedom, and prosperity, then the only rational way to do so is to back the standing President of the United States. There will be no other alternative for us. This election year, we cannot afford to lose what we have worked so hard to get. It is time we as Americans put the Democrats and the Liberals packing. Vote for President Trump now; vote for President Trump to keep this country and world safe.

Chapter 5

JOBS, JOBS, AND MORE JOBS.

TRUMP WILL CREATE MORE JOBS.

Whether you are rich or poor, pretty or ugly, you have the same basic human needs. You want to find love, you want to belong, you want to be able to put food on your table, and you want to raise your kids in a great country where there are opportunities to be free and to live freely. This is perhaps the desire of all mankind. You want a job. Really. The Bible tells us we need to work. Do you notice that everyone can work, unless they are not physically able to do so, or the person is mentally challenged? Aside from that, people want to work and they should work. I have yet to meet anyone who wasn't looking for a job, or looking to get a better job, or looking to create more wealth, and so they wouldn't work as hard. Working is like a standard and you feel good about yourself when you do.

President Trump works hard; he is in his 70s and is still working. It is unlikely that Trump will ever retire. Trump understands that work is important to humans and it is unhealthy not to work. I am black and so I should know that. I have a lot of black friends who live on welfare and I can tell you, the longer they live on welfare, the more negative and gloomy they become. Why is that? Because the human body was not devised to not work. If you read the 12 steps for alcoholics, one of the basic ways to keep addiction astray is to put people to work. In fact, most people would put themselves into trouble if they didn't work. Work is good for you and you must not let anyone tell you otherwise. I do understand that not everyone is making 100,000 per year, but the money is relative. It is the movement, human contact, and the use of the brain or hands that is important. This is why the Bible tells us to do everything with all our heart and to work with all our heart. The Bible has never told anyone to retire or to live off the government. It is not biblical and it is not a natural human response, and so you should never let the government take your working power from you. Why? Because once you go on the government programs, you will get addicted to the free stuff and will lose all your incentive to work. This is all a trick to control you. The only reason the government wants you not to work is that they want to steal from you. If we depend on the government to take care of us, the government people (politicians such as Bernie Sanders, Elizabeth Warren, and Joe Biden) will always have a job. Don't you see what the Democrats are doing to us? They are promising us everything for free. Basically, they are saying "I will always have a job and you people won't"; I will print all the money in the world, and you will no longer need to work. Free is addictive. If you stop working you surely will become lazy and the Democrats are betting on this. How do I know? Because I think in the same lines as these people since I am a lawyer and I can see what they are doing to you. And so I am writing this book to expose the truth about the ugliest of politicians. I want people to know that being a lawyer is not an honorable profession. There are a lot of crooked lawyers out there and you already know that. Unfortunately, most of the crooked lawyers are now your politicians. Some of them are even running for office and want to be your next President. Please don't trust those crooked lawyers. I finally can see where all these lawyer jokes come from. It is sickening to watch lawyers such as Sanders, Biden, and Elizabeth Warren go to Washington D.C. and scam people for a living. Sanders, Biden, and Warren are scamming us, the taxpayers, who have to vote. Biden, Sanders, and Warren are promising us a life where we will never have to work. If it is so good, why aren't their families living on the welfare system? Why are their families working? Don't be fooled by them—Sanders' wife works, Biden's wife works, and Warren's husband works. None of them are living on the welfare system. Think about it. Why is it that they want jobs, but they don't want you to have one? Do not be fooled by them. Biden, Sanders, and Warren do not want you to work because they want to ensure that they have a job for the rest of their lives. The more people depend on free stuff, the more the people (politicians such as Sanders, Warren, and Biden) at the top get power. If Sanders, Biden, or Warren win the Oval office, and they start printing money and make us not work, then what do you think is going to happen? We are going to have to depend upon free for the rest of our lives, which makes it obvious that we are going to need those politicians in office for the rest of their lives. So you see, Biden, Warren, and Sanders and all those other Democrats are trying to sell themselves to you. They want to stay in power forever and they want you to pay for their lifestyle. How do you do that you ask? When you stop working, you stop thinking for yourself, and you allow the politicians to take care of you for the rest of your life. In exchange, these politicians and their families will always have a job, and you will just be at their mercy. How can this be a good deal? Right now you are free to work. You can get qualified and land any job you want. If that doesn't work for you, luckily you live in America, where you can go ahead and create your own darn job. I am not bragging but I started my law firm with around $1400.00 in my bank account. I didn't fear anything. I was a brand new lawyer who went to a third-tier law school and landed a job that paid me $30,000 per year. I didn't think I deserved that little bit of money, and so I branched out with 1400 and started my own law firm. I cannot say that I have become rich from it, but yes, I can say that it provides food for me and my children and I have a roof over my head. I think that is plenty for me considering that I am self-employed. I am only

43 years old and I thank God that I live in America as a black woman and that I can go to work and feed my two kids and myself. I am not looking to make millions like other people, I am just looking to be happy. I would be very unhappy if I do not get to work and the politicians take away my right to have a job. When I wasn't happy with my job, I knew I had a choice; I could either keep that job, create my own job, or find another job that made me happy. I think most Americans are like me. I have a 25-year-old niece who had changed her jobs a few times before finally finding one that made her happy and she is currently pursuing it. We do have a lot of freedom in America if you look at it.

I mean, we get to choose where we live, what clothes to wear, what job to do, what car to drive, and whom to marry. Why would you give up your freedom to some random politician who gives you a few soundbites about free? If the welfare system and not working is so good, why don't those politicians give up their jobs, go live of the welfare system for a few years, and then come back and report to us just how much fun it is. Don't you see this is just a bull crap story? A bunch of lawyers figured a way to become crooked politicians and the money is so sweet that they want to figure a way to keep the scheme going. So, they come to sell us a story on living for free. It sounds good at first, but you must understand, what is in store for the politicians and what really is in store for you?

I know a thing or two about addiction. What is addiction?

When you are addicted to something, you cannot stop yourself from doing it. Getting everything for free is a form of addiction, which is why once people stop working they are not able to get back to work because they become addicted to not working. The politicians know this, and this is why when the Democrats came into power they immediately increased all the free spending and welfare benefits they possible could. They want you to be on their payroll because that way they (Democrat) will become indispensable. You will need someone to keep the payroll afloat and so you are now forced to keep voting for the man who promised you freedom. As we become more of a welfare country, the government will grow bigger and bigger. The rich people will either jump ship and go to other countries in the world where they won't be taxed as much; or better yet, some wealthy people will buy very expensive yachts and they will figure a way to live in the international waters forever. That way they will never be subject to any government taxes. If you read the Bible, it is plain simple that there will always be a group that is wealthy, there will always be a group that is poor, and there will always be a group that is middle class. Do not let this divide us my friend and do not let the politicians let you think being poor is a crime, because it is not! What is a crime is being lazy, which in itself is an abomination to the Lord (quote the Bible verses on this). Do not let any politician take away your talent. There is nothing wrong with sweeping the floors or waiting on food tables. Any form of work is work, the main concept being serving others. You get to connect with other people and you are forced to serve them. If you do not work, how will you serve? If you are on welfare all day, how will you serve others? It is more than likely that you will just go home and watch TV all day because there will be nothing to do. You will stress more because your income will be fixed on Washington D.C and you will get a cheque only when Washington D.C. chooses to send you one. What if these same government people decide they no longer want to fund the welfare system and after 10 years of being on welfare and having no jobs, you all will have to go out and work. How is that going to work out for you? Won't it be horrible? A part of my responsibility as a lawyer is just to educate people in the community. I meet people all the time who had fallen on hard times due to some addiction. These people overcome their addiction after years of fighting and then they cannot get a decent job. Do you know why? It is because they have been out of the workforce for years and over this time the technologies and the talent requirements have changed. As such, these people are no longer able to keep up. Do not give up your job for free money. You are not doing yourself a favor but are instead becoming a learned helpless on whom the Democratic party will prey upon. You need a job to be functional and to contribute to society. You need a job to give your children an example of what it is like to go out and get work and become something in society. If we all live for free, who will take our garbage out? Who will teach our kids? Who will see us when we get sick? Do you see how senseless this sounds? We cannot have a community where no one works. We need a community where everyone works and this is why I am a Republican. I do not need good soundbites to make me feel good. You tell me to work and I am going to work. Like everyone else, I don't always like my work but I do it anyway. There are some days when work is more stressful than the other days, but that is no excuse for not doing work. Work must be done no matter what. I tell my kids every day that if we do not work, we will not be able to eat. I am not waiting for the government to hand me down something because we make more when we do our own work. Do not let any government send you a cheque in exchange for you not working. That government entity will own you for life. I know it is not the intention of any voter to give away his/her power to a bunch of crooked lawyers running for office on the Democratic ticket. Do yourself a favor and vote for President Donald J. Trump to be re-elected come November 2020.

Chapter 6

WITH TRUMP, THE FUTURE FOR AMERICA LOOKS GOOD.

America, your future is bright with President Trump by your side. You can feel Trump's energy in the air. I had the great opportunity to attend a rally where President Trump spoke. What I can tell you is that when he talks, you know that it makes sense. When Trump speaks, you know it is from his heart. Ladies and gentlemen, why take a chance to remove a wonderful President from the office with some radical idea from the left. Do you see who the Democrats have running against President Trump? I don't think one of those Democrats even has a fighting chance in a dog fight, let alone to hold an office as high as the Oval office.

One thing I have learned while living in this country—this wonderful country we call America—is that if you believe something, and you act upon it, then it will happen. It is now time for the blacks to come out and vote as never before. You need to get out and vote for President Trump and the Republican party. Why? If you don't, we are going to see the ripple effect of a bad economy. We cannot trust who the Liberals have in their back pockets. There is not one strong party on the Democrat's side that is worth a second look. Why reinvent the Wheel when things are working and looking up for us now? If we do not back our standing President, then all those dreams of a bright future might just be taken away. America, let's not take a chance of voting for any Liberal agenda. Let's get together and get our votes out for President Donald J. Trump.

Do you remember when President Obama was in office? The country felt weird. The country had the biggest recession of all time. I am sure you either lost your home or you knew someone who had lost their home during the biggest foreclosure crisis of all time. President Obama and all the Liberals including all the Democrats who are now running for office against President Trump are responsible for that great loss. Why would you want to go back in time? If the Democrats did it to us once, they will surely do it again. This will belly up the country and the future of coming generations. It is not worth taking a chance. I hope that I am driving the truth inside of you real good because come election night, 2020, a lot is at stake. I have worked in the political field in the past and I have had the privilege of working on some major political campaigns. I took a break when I had my children. I feel blessed that my five-year-old twins live in this beautiful country America, but I got to tell you something. I am just like you. I stay up at night and quietly worry about my children's and grandchildren's future. And I know that we can do better. I believe, and you will agree with me, that President Donald Trump is the perfect President to lead this country in the right direction. There is so much progress being made right now, wouldn't it be unwise to disturb the momentum? I think, as citizens of this great country, our duty now is to re-elect Trump and sit back and watch how things work out for us. I feel with President Trump your future, your kid's future, and your grandchildren's future will be really bright. Why don't you just keep it this way? Do not back down. It is time for us to back the sitting President.

Chapter 7

A Tale of Two Parties.

With President Trump and the Republican party, there seems to be a race to bring America to the top. We see the President already doing that. With the Democratic party, there is always a race to the bottom. The Democrats would love Americans to be as dumb as a doornail. That way we can all depend upon the government's spending. The Democrats would like us to stop thinking for ourselves, after all, that might just be too much work for one human to do. Would you like someone to tell you how much food you can feed your child? Would you like someone to tell you how much exercise you need? Would you like someone to just control all of your life? Would you like it if you won't be able to make any decisions? Well, if you follow the Democrats, that is the position they wish to take the Americans. The Democrats believe that Americans are too stupid to think for themselves, and only the very few at the top (crooked rich politicians such as Bernie Sanders) are the ones who can think for us. Knowledge is power. The more we can kick the government out of our lives, the freer we will be. Most of the negative in the air comes from the political climate. There are reasons why people get involved in politics, and one of them is for making real changes that will make this world and country a better place to live in. This is where President Trump comes in. President Trump has the black people's agenda; he has all the people's agenda. Why take a chance with someone else. Do everyone and yourself a favor and go out this coming election cycle and vote for Donald J. Trump.

Chapter 8

WE HAVE BEEN LIED TO WAY TOO LONG.

Blacks, I am talking to you. I might not be able to reach to all the blacks, but I know I can reach the blacks who are under and around the age of 50. I can also reach the Caribbean blacks. I think it is time for us blacks to stop accepting the lies we have been told time and again. I remember when I was 19, I had attended an event where I was called the N word. I didn't think much of it. After all, I spent most of my time being raised in Jamaica—a country where being black is nothing. So when someone called me the N word, I was a bit puzzled. I wondered if it was to mean something. However, I didn't care because, by the time I was living in America, I was too ambitious to care that the color of my skin was not the right color to succeed. I remember being in places such as Aspen Colorado around the age of 27, and people stared at me because I knew how to ski. They all wondered how a black person could ski. The problem we have in this country as a black person is we let the Liberal media, the Al Sharpton and the Jesse Jackson of the world, define who we are. As blacks, we have been told there are no jobs. As blacks we have been told to fight the police. As blacks we have been told to join gangs. I am sure most whites do not understand the blacks and black crimes. Every other nationality understands that blacks have a crab in the barrel mentality. In other words, if you as a black person start to be successful, the other blacks are supposed to knock you back down from your success. I got to tell you this. I do not mean to stereotype but the Chinese, the whites, and the Jewish people do not behave in that manner. When my partner and I were getting ready to buy a home, we wanted a home in a good school district. My partner is white and I am black and so we have mixed kids. My partner asked his friend for some advice for the school district and I remember saying to myself, "Wow. How can you trust your friend? What if he gives you information to the wrong school district?" I watch the interaction of my partner and his other white friends, and I can tell you, it is not the relationship that blacks keep. Even when I attended Law school, there were less than 10 black people in my class of 60, and you know what, they didn't really get along. There was always that I need to beat you out type of thing. Have you noticed as a black person when you move in the area, the other blacks get upset? It is time for us blacks to love being around each other. It is time for us blacks to not let politics, big civic leaders, and other corporations divide us. Do you know why they divide us? Because when you divide a group, you conquer the group. And this is why blacks will always oppress blacks. You won't see a Jewish group oppressing another Jewish group. It is only the blacks who love to divide themselves. The Bible said a house divided cannot stand. It is time for us blacks to unite and get behind the Republican agenda. You see, the Republican agenda is the black's agenda. The Republicans believe in creating jobs. Who doesn't want to work? Every person who works feels good about himself. It doesn't matter if you wash a table cloth or sweep the floor, work raises the self-esteem of any person. This is why the Bible has no place in there for retirement. Nowhere in the Bible does it say that you must work and then someday retire. Do you know why? Because God designed our bodies and he knows our bodies are designed to work. I have been unemployed a few times in this country. Sadly, when I had my children, I had to take time away from work to care for them. I love my children, but it wasn't a good feeling for me to not get a paycheck weekly. Don't get me wrong. Being a housewife is a full-time job, and it is a job that doesn't pay; so, your hats must go off to all the housewives. But here I am talking about healthy able persons who just don't work. You know when you stay home, you start getting lazy. To cope with your laziness, you start doing drugs or become an alcoholic. And before you know it, you are not able to work again. It is good to work; if it wasn't, how do you explain wealthy people becoming politicians. This is because people understand that without work you won't have much meaning to life. You need something to challenge you. You need an avenue to talk with random people every day and that is how you grow. Working is Biblical. If you ever become a Christian, and you get to read your Bible, you will see clearly that a job is important. How could you not like a President who promises to help you fulfill your human destination? President Trump and the Republican party promise to bring jobs to America. The Democrats are not the same; they promise to get rid of jobs and create a system where the government will just send us a paycheck every month. Please tell me how will this benefit you in the long run. When you have a job, you get the flexibility of getting paid more. When the government sends you a cheque monthly, you cannot tell the government "That is it! I quit! I need more money!" The government will do as it pleases. Why would you give power to a bunch of knuckleheads? Have you heard some of these politicians' speeches before? Some of these Democrats cannot even point a finger on the map on where America is, let alone control the destination of 400 million people. Come on, this is the reality! This is not a reality show. We need to vote for President Trump—the maker of American jobs. Don't waste your vote on some Liberal politician; keep things simple, keep things right! Just go out and vote in this 2020 election for President Donald J. Trump.

Chapter 9

GOVERNMENT SERVES ITS PEOPLE. PEOPLE DO NOT SERVE THE GOVERNMENT.

Right in our very eyes, there is a battle between the big government and the small government. The Democrats would love the government to keep growing because they think that with a big government and a huge income to spend they can serve the people better. Do you like people giving you 100 rules or 10 rules? Do you love freedom or do you love slavery? Here is why the Liberal media and the Democrats want to grow the government. The bigger the government, the more power gets transferred from the people to the government. Think about that. This is why the Democrats are trying to give us everything for free. People such as Senator Elizabeth Warren, U.S representative Cortez, U.S. Senator Bernie Sanders, and the bunch of Liberals running for President plan to cripple the power from the people. Most of the politicians in America are lawyers. I am a lawyer too and I know how lawyers think. Sadly, I am not always proud of my profession because lawyers write the law and they themselves make sure that there are loopholes so they won't have to follow the rules. These very same lawyers then perfect the loopholes and run for office. And what happens next? They get so used to the free money from politics that they do not want it to stop. So they decide to trick people into not working, not caring about taking care of themselves, and not being creative. They just keep getting people to depend less and less on themselves (the people) and more and more on the government. The more we the people depend on the government, the worst off we will be. Have you ever been to Europe? I have been going perhaps once per year for the past seven years of my life. I have a bunch of relatives who live in England and so I go there during the summer and shoot the breeze with them. I do not think I could live in Europe. It is too much of a socialist country. What makes me say that? Well, look at this. In Europe, you cannot just start a business. It is not that super easy. Rather, you better be coming from money and that is plenty of money. In America, anyone with a driver's license and a little common sense can start a business. Don't you see how blessed we are here in this country? We are able to start a business that can actually feed our family and this is just one of the greatest things we can do in America. I would say when there is a Republican President, business owners tend to thrive, and I do not mean thrive as in making money. I have the pleasure of talking with business owners every single day because as a business owner myself, I have to work with other business owners. And what I can tell you is that a business' success is not always measured by the money it makes. Just owning a business is a success in itself because we are finally able to do what we want. I am afraid all of that will be lost if we have a Democrat in the office.

Chapter 10

Do yourself A Favor, Vote for Trump and the Republican Party Come November 2020.

When was the last time you treated yourself to something you really deserved? You know it is hard sometimes as humans to just do something that is good for us. After all, society has brainwashed us into even thinking that taking a five-day vacation is just too much of a stretch. But the truth is, it is not! You deserve it! This is the same as the Republican party and President Trump. Ladies and gentlemen of America, President Trump is good for this country. You and I both know that. While I write this book, I am looking at the stock market and all I can see is the Americans are getting richer thanks to President Trump. I know most Americans don't own stocks, but most of these stocks are responsible for the pensions that most Americans will be getting. So indirectly, even if you do not own even one share of stock, chances are the company you worked for has invested in the stock market. And if you were able to obtain a 401k, then considered yourself blessed, as the money is now pouring into your coffer. Let's go back in time to when President Trump ran and won the election in 2016. Remember how shocked the Liberal media and the democratic party was? Do you recall Hillary Clinton had felt that she won the election and would be the next President? But what happened? People, voters, smart voters like you did exactly what was supposed to be done. You went into the voting booth and you voted for President Trump. Of course, when the pollers asked people who they would vote for, the voters didn't give these silly pollsters the right response. This is because people knew darn well that they deserve a good country. People understood darn well that they deserve to pay lesser taxes. People understood darn well that they deserve a smaller government. People understood darn well that only President Trump and the Republican party could keep this country safe. And the voters went inside that voting booth and voted with their hearts and their minds. The voters voted for President Trump and the Republican party, and this my friend is why we have such a great country. People understand they deserve better and people want good. So if you want good, you know who to vote for—obviously, President Trump and the Republican party. It is the best choice to get good treatment, and you deserve nothing but the best. President Trump and the Republican party only wants what is good for the American people and America, so, why wouldn't you just come on board for that?

So my next question to you as voters is why is voting for President Trump such a treat. And you know what a treat is? How do you reward yourself for your hard work, or if you exercise? You treat yourself to something nice. You know what I mean. Let me bring you back to those days when you treated yourself. You know like you just got a job promotion you would treat yourself to a nice bottle or glass of wine with your friends because you celebrated that journey and you darn well knew that you deserved that promotion. You worked hard and nothing good was being held from you. You got out of debt and you were able to purchase a luxury car, such as a large pink long Mercedes Benz with a flat room, white and pink leather interior, and a loud stereo. That is a real treat because you worked so hard to do the right thing and now you are being rewarded. Or for example, when you have finally lost 10 pounds from running 10 miles per week and went to the large loud beautiful mall in America, walked into one of those stores, and tried on the most amazing black silk dress. You know that dress you always wanted to wear but you believed you didn't have the body to wear it? Now you could treat yourself to that because you had worked hard to get it and you deserved that dress. Well, think of President Trump and the Republican party that way. President Trump is a real treat to America. We have worked hard for years and we cannot see where we are going. I talk to people every single day; people from all walks of life. I have talked to the middle class, the poor, and the rich, and one thing sure is common among them all—everyone likes a good treat. Everyone understands that he/she deserves more. His/her child/children deserve a better future. His/her child/children deserve a better education system. He/she deserves better health care than the silly ones we get from Government handouts, such as Obamacare. He/she deserves a job promotion regardless of his/her ethnicity. He/she deserves to live in a better America. And that is what President Trump reiterates. President Trump is the real treat we need. We deserve the best and President Trump is the best in terms of resume and job skills. I mean how often are we so blessed to have a billionaire run our country. Don't you see? President Trump is over-qualified for the job of being a President. So why wouldn't you vote for him? President Trump is used to a salary of millions of dollars per year, while the President of the United States only gets paid $400,000 per year. It was never designed for a billionaire to become a President. After all, how would the founder father have figured out we could have attracted such good talent. President Trump is great for this country in another way too. Being inspired by him, other rich and other businessmen will follow suit, which will be a welcome change to the lawyers who run our country. Most people hate lawyers running our country, and what better way than this to break from that mold.

TRUMP LOOKS STRONG TO THE WORLD LEADERS

Do you want a weak leader or a strong leader? Do you want the world to feel sorry for you or do you want the world to be afraid of you? I am writing this while I am in a hotel in London, England and I feel good about this discussion because I know what I look like overseas. When I tell people I come from the United States of America, I can see how they look at me with pride. They know my leader President Donald J. Trump is a strong man, and they know that America is a strong country. I hope you get the point. People across the world won't be able to easily mess with you. Why? Because you have a President who is strong, and if we as Americans get messed with, President Trump will have no problem in making those countries pay for their grave mistake. Have you ever been spoiled when you were growing up? Did you have a mother or father who would give you a candy before you eat your dinner? Or if you didn't like the dinner, you didn't have to eat it anyway and nothing would come of it. Your parents you know loved you and sometimes they just spoiled you. Well, think of President Trump that way. Trump is the type of President who loves his country, America. No matter how bad we are as Americans, he is going to make us look good to the world. Wouldn't you rather have a President who gives you everything than someone like Bernie Sanders, Joe Biden, or Elizabeth Warren and the remaining Liberals who give you nothing and take everything from you? You know what I am talking about. Just go to the black areas in America and ask people if they have a relative in jail? The answer I am sure will be yes. Why? Because Democrats such as Clinton, Sanders, Warren and Biden punish blacks all the time. This is why the only president reform we ever got came from President Trump. I am going to touch more on being black in America because this is serious. We cannot have young blacks going to jail when some of them just need more help due to their mental illness.

Do you remember having siblings and being the preferred child sometimes by your mother or father? The world is not perfect because there is good and evil and this is how life is. So look, we live in an unfair system, but we blacks who live in America are much better off than those who live in Africa. So why wouldn't you just get the best leader in the World to lead you? If someone offers you a 2016 Honda Accord or a 2016 Mercedes Benz for free, which one would you choose? Wouldn't you take the better one? So when you are looking at the Presidential candidates, look at them as a brand, because that is what it is. Look at their resumes. Look at who is making billions of dollars and has been creating jobs in the private and public sector for most of their adult lives. Look at who has been working 12 hours a day for 5 – 6 days per week. Who is a better leader that can stand up to a big government? The answer is President Donald J. Trump. Don't be stupid! Treat yourself to a damn good President because we deserve the best. It is time for us to stop selling ourselves short and just pick the best man to lead this country. Come November 2020, get to the voting polls and vote to re-elect President Donald J. Trump.

Black Americans need Trump

Yes, I said it. I had to title this chapter or discussion in this way because I have to address the elephant in the room. It is time for the Blacks to jump off the Democratic train and come over to the Republicans. Blacks, do yourself a favor by voting for Trump. The Democratic party has already betrayed you, so might as well, we as blacks, betray them. I am a lawyer working down in South Florida. I have met a lot of black people through my law practice, church, and just with the sheer luck of being black. I can tell you that blacks are hurting in this country. There are mothers like me, with kids. These mothers need to work two to three jobs to make ends meet. These blacks mothers either have a husband who is not working (this is acceptable in the black community) or he is just her child's baby father, who she is sharing with another woman. Yes, I am saying it. Come write to me later when I am done publishing and selling this book. The sad part of being black in America is that you or your loved ones will be jailed or killed. Jail for blacks is a better option than being killed because at least, when you are jailed, you will lose time, but you will get some for yourself. But if you are killed, that's the end of it. But here is the unfairness towards blacks in America. What if I tell you that 70% of the blacks who are in jail in America are there because they came from a broken home. What is a broken home? A home where the father is not involved because he might be in jail himself or he is being shared by another woman or two. A broken home is when the only male role is a black mother who needs to work three jobs to feed her three kids. So, how will she have the time to come home and tell her son not to join a gang, when she is busy hustling to put food on the table? This is a catch 22 here. Do you get the point? Keep reading. You will see the reality of blacks in America. For a single black mother to put food on the table, she must work three jobs, which means around 12 to 14 hours of shift per day for five to seven days every week. Do you get what I am saying? A broken home is when your options are limited. As such, what must a black boy in America do to become a man? He must go out and prove himself to the world? And how does a black boy in America prove himself to the world? Well, remember everyone's world is different. In the black man's world, a gang member is the king, while in a white man's world, the CEO is the king. I am showing you how different the world we live in is and how different people operate. So the black little boys whose mother works three jobs because she has no husband and she refuses to let her kids starve, her son, feel they can make something of themselves if they just join the gang and then they can go higher up in ranking. Well, you and I both know this kind of thinking doesn't work out. If you join a gang, you are going to end up being killed or jailed. If you get higher up the ranks, you will be doing a lot of killing, and so all you are doing is absorbing negative energy, which will lead to negative karma. The Bible tells us we reap what we sow. Do not think that joining a gang will bring any good to anyone's life. I do not care if you are in the Ghetto. You must choose other options, and being a gang member is not one of them. (However, that is for a different book.) I am just trying to show you that we are closer to solving the gang problems in America as it all lies in the hands of the Republican party and President Donald J. Trump. Please read on to see what I am talking about.

When it comes to gang members, especially black kids, we are talking about young naive kids who have no father role. So, naturally, if a gang member approaches such kids and tells them that they will be a star someday, as young kids they will believe it. It is just like what white people tell their kids every morning. Go to school and work hard so that you can become anything you want. Well, these young white kids believe it and this is why I went to law school with so many white people. It had been instilled in them as little kids to go to law school, believe in themselves, and become lawyers.

But in the ghetto, unfortunately, there aren't many role models. There is a lot of negativity in the ghetto because most of the people there are hurt. There are broken homes; there is poverty. You cannot feel good about being both poor and in a broken home. This is all the evil that is being spread in the ghetto, and so, the young black boys, who come from broken homes, join gangs to feel accepted because as humans we feel the need to be accepted. This is why we have a family, and this is why when we leave our parents' home we look for a partner or a mate. We just want to feel accepted. This is why people divorce someone they loved for someone they have fallen in love with now. It is all because they want to feel accepted. In the ghetto too, the little black boys are trying to be. They too want a family. But, unfortunately, the little black boys do what they are told by the gang leaders and then these young black boys end up in jail. If you kill someone or you hurt someone, you will for sure go to jail. There will be no gang member who will protect you from that. The system punishes these young black boys in a very harsh way. Rather than trying to get to the root cause of what is going wrong with the family and strengthen the family ties, the system (government, big leaders of the government such as Sanders, Biden, and Warren) punish the blacks by putting their children, these little black boys, into jail. Do you think this is fair? No, it is not a fair system! These little black boys do not deserve to be trapped in this system for the rest of their lives all because they have no father figure. These little black boys do not deserve to be in jail for the rest of their lives all because when they were little they tried to survive in the ghetto by joining the gang. These little black boys do not deserve to be in jail for the rest of their lives, all because people like Obama, Sanders, Biden, Clinton, Warrant, and the Democratic party failed them. No sir or ma'am, they don't! We need to make sure that these black little boys get justice and the only way we can do so is by voting for President Donald J. Trump. In this way, we can keep the prison reform going on and we can bring more meaning to others in jail and we will have a way to reach out to them and get them out.

Let me add more insult to injury here. Do you know it is even easier for blacks to be prosecuted than whites here in America under the federal or state criminal justice system? Yikes, I said it! I am a lawyer and I see it every day. I am here to tell you the reality of the justice system. I am sorry, I am not criticizing it but I have to speak the truth. If not, I am just full of crap like all the other crooked lawyers out there in America. Do you know why it is so easy to convict a black man or a black boy in America?

Because the Liberal media and Hollywood make movies that you and I both watch. And what are these movies about? These movies portray blacks as being violent and evil, and perception is reality. That is how simple life is. Guess what happens next, people who watch a lot of television someday become juries. What do you think these juries do? They just prosecute the blacks much easier because that is what they (people who watch Liberal television) are doing. People who are juries act out based on what they see on television because they believe that what is shown on television must somehow be the reality. This is what Liberal television has shown us over the years. It shows us to stereotype. It stereotypes blacks as poor, stupid, ignorant, killers, and crooks. So, how easy is it to prosecute a black in this country you ask? Too easy. It is as easy as taking candy from a sleeping baby. And the Democrats call this justice! But then, guess what has happened now?

The world is beginning to change in terms of how people perceive different races. The younger generation are intermingling with blacks. Celebrities and pop-cultures are marrying into black families. Think Kim Kardashian and Kayne West. And now, when things affect the rich blacks or the whites with black families, what do they do? They fight back? (There really are no changes in America unless it affects people with money or people who have power—we will touch on that later on).

Then came the Prison Reform that was spearheaded by Kardashian and Jared Kushner, Trump's son-in-law. Because Trump is so wealthy, he cannot and won't see black versus white because, in a rich man's world, he looks at talent. He never looks at a man's color. How do I know? Because I have very wealthy clients who hired me because of my gift and not the color of my skin. I practice law in Palm Beach. Palm Beach is perhaps one of the most wealthy communities in the entire world. I do not have the wealth these people have but I am exposed to wealthy clients on a daily basis because of my law practice; after all, I am in Palm

Beach. When it wasn't popular to be black in this country, I was a young black lawyer making money in Palm Beach. The majority of my clients were rich white men and women, who didn't care that I was black. They cared that I had talent. I would go to their 10 million dollar homes and I would be the only black there, but they didn't care! All they cared about was that I was able to conduct my real estate transactions that would earn them money. If I was incompetent in making them money, they would fire me. It was the first time that I understood a lesson in this country. When it comes to the rich, they love to surround themselves with talent or other rich people. And the rich, including President Donald Trump, won't give a rat ass if you are black, white, Chinese, or Indian. As long as you have a talent that a rich man could use, you would be part of that rich man business team. This is why when I was growing up my parents used to beat me to study my books. Yes, I grew up in a very conservative home with a mother and father who dragged me to church every single Sunday of my life. (I still going to church perhaps two Sundays per month now and I feel guilty for not going every single Sunday). I had a mother and father who sent me to private school, not to show off but to make sure I was in a smaller class and I could learn better. I had a mother and father who would malice me if I didn't have good grades. Yes, my black mother and my black father would not talk to me if I came home with Fs and not As. Even if I used to get two Cs, my parents would not talk to me. I never understood it until I got older. My mother used to say to me "Education will levy the playing field for you. If you want to live in America, you need to be educated." And that is the only way as a black person you can be taken seriously. That was in my time, but I am already 43 now. Today the situation is different; it is a different time. I summered in the Hamptons for the last five years; I am very blessed that way. I have seen little 10-year-old rich white kids listening to black music and they also have black friends now. The world is changing. The world will change in our very eyes but we still have work to do in the black communities. We need to get those blacks who have mental illnesses out of jail and put into the proper programs. And I am afraid that Sanders, Biden, Warren, and the rest of those running under the Democratic ticket will do nothing. I am afraid as a black person living in this white country that the democrat party, including the main ring leaders such as Sanders, Biden, and Warren, might want to put chains back on the blacks. They won't send us back to Africa but they will enslave us here in America. How do I know that? Because we voted for the so-call black Presidents Clinton and Obama, and there was no prison reform then. Warren, Biden, and Sanders and all the other Democrat people running for office today have yet to say anything about the Prison reform. The democrat's silence speaks volume. It means the black agenda is a dead agenda to the Democratic party. So why bother to waste time? You can just be like me and other young blacks, who are voting for Donald J. Trump for President of the United States. We are voting for all the Republicans on the November 2020 election ticket. Why? Because Trump already started Prison reform that is going to help the black community. Why not let him get another 4 years to kill the prison system? That way more blacks will be free and they will go home to their families.

THE REALITY OF BLACKS AND MENTAL ILLNESS IN THIS COUNTRY; ONLY TRUMP CAN HELP THIS MENTAL ILLNESS CRISIS.

You do not need to agree with me but I am giving you some facts here. I know reality is never easy to comprehend. This is why most people want to get high for most of their lives. They are just sick of seeing the reality in life. Do you know that most black men who are in jail have some form of mental illness? How do I know that? Because I am a lawyer and I speak with people who commit crimes all the time. They have one thing in common—they could all get a mental illness diagnosis whether it is alcoholism, high functioning autism, attention deficit disorder (ADD or ADHD).

MOST BLACKS ARE IN JAIL BECAUSE OF MENTAL ILLNESS

Blacks, we can make a difference together. You might be asking how? Simple, we are stronger in numbers. How are we stronger in numbers? If we vote for Trump, when he wins, we can make our demands for mental illness or the other issues blacks face. How would that work? Because we become voters? Why do you think that the seniors or elder people in Florida are so important to politicians? Because those people vote. Remember, you only get heard if the politicians can see you. If you do not vote, then whatever issue keeps you up at night won't get addressed. How will President Trump know that mental illness is a problem in the black community if any black leaders haven't told him so? How will President Trump know that the black people want a seat at his table if he doesn't see them often at the rallies? You need to speak up and the only way to speak up is to go get involved in the political process. You need to go to President Trump's rallies and other republican rallies and listen to what they have to say. You need to follow President Trump's web pages and his agenda and get involved. Then, when the republican party sees enough of us (blacks around), we will let them know what we want. We want a better future for all races. We want better jobs for all our families. We want more wealth to be created and preserved for all our families and for the generations to come after us. We want equal rights like every other person in the World. And we will speak up. Do you know why I am speaking up about mental health issues? Because I meet enough blacks who are mentally ill and I meet enough blacks whose families are in jail because of mental illness. I am a black living in America long enough to know that the issue of blacks being in jail because of mental illness must be addressed. Do you know a lot of blacks are in jail because they are mentally ill? I said it. Many black men are in jail in the United States of America because they suffer some form of mental illness. Mental illness is a big stigma in the black community. When a white person gets sick, his parents or caregivers get him into rehab and the professionals take care of things for that white person. Eventually, that white person is able to go back into the community with medicine and therapy on his side, and live a normal productive life. You wouldn't even know this white person is on medicines. Because after all, if someone is on Xanax, it isn't broadcast through his clothes. On the other hand, the black community just avoids mental illness because they believe it is madness. If someone black has bi-polar, he will not take his medicine because he will be stigmatized. Unfortunately, some of these blacks in jail are suffering from mental illness and they are not getting the same treatment as whites. Rather than going to rehab and working things out through therapy, a black person is more prone to acting out his mental illness on the street with crime and then ending up in jail. Why should a black mentally-ill person go to jail for mental illness and a white person go to rehab? If we are all created equal, then blacks must demand to get these black men and women out of jail and into rehab for their mental illness. Anyone with mental illness is capable of living a productive life if he or she receives medicine and or therapy. Having mental illness, whether you are black or white, is not a death sentence. In fact, with medicine, knowledge, and technology improving so rapidly, a person with mental illness can do just fine. We need to address mental illness in the political arena because we need the funding and the legal protection that the Federal Government can give us in releasing the blacks from jail, and throwing money into invocation, rehab, and other treatment for mental illness. We can do this by educating ourselves on the political field and voting for President Donald J. Trump come

November 2020. Then, we can address these things by forming grass root efforts on mental illness. People think I am optimistic and I sure am. I travel a lot and I can see the energy, the vibes, and the momentum of people in this Country. Things are looking up for us because President Donald J. Trump is strong in America. I think the picking is ripe for blacks to start tackling mental illness. Timing is everything. I did not see a time like this before; blacks are now ready to take on the subject of mental illness. I think with Celebrities such as Kayne West being diagnosis with Bi-polar and other black celebrities that suffer some setbacks because of mental illness, the other blacks are now ready to speak up about it. I also believe that there are finally plenty of young black people who do not have a stigma on the white population. After all, these young blacks are growing up in a house where multi-culture families are now the norm. I can see the changes in my own family. Most of my relatives under the age of 30 are black coming home from college and get married to a white person. It is nothing these days for a young white man to have a black wife, which is wonderful. We are all created in the image of God and He does not see color, only man sees color. Someday, I am going to be able to write that man no longer sees color because that day will come soon in America and I have a feeling it will be in our lifetime. I think these young black people are willing to listen and take other approach that the only generation. I think young blacks understand that mental illness has its stigma, but with proper treatment, anyone with a mental illness can live a productive life. Jail is not where a mentally-ill person needs to be. If jail is to rehabilitate people for their crimes, then you have to rehabilitate the mentally-ill in rehab. In this way, proper treatment and therapy can help this black mentally-ill person live a productive life. "A mind is a terrible thing to waste." according to the Slogan of United Negro College Fund. There are plenty of mad people but very few functional people in society. People should contribute to society because the Bible tells us to work and, we need to understand that a mentally-ill person in jail is capable of coming out of jail and living a productive life with the right treatment and therapy. Trump can make this a reality for us because we have seen that Trump is already open to Prison Reform. We see mental illness topics being taken on these days. It is time that we as blacks jump on the Trump train and vote to re-elect President Donald J. Trump come November 2020. So far it seems President Donald J Trump is the only person willing to listen to the blacks and provide Prison Reform, might as well, we expand that topic by dashing mental illness into it. But we cannot do so without the votes. So you as a black person, as a voter, as a Christian need to get out and vote come November 2020 for the re-election of President Donald J. Trump.

CHRISTIANITY AND THE REPUBLICAN PARTY

Most Christians do not want to get involved in politics. They are more focused on a spiritual journey here on earth than anything else. You know the Christians I am talking about. They go to church two times per week. They work their jobs. They get married. They have a family. They praise and worship God every single day. They witness to people around them but that is about it. They won't go to political rallies and that is okay. But some Christians have been called to be in politics and they know who they are. I believe I am one of those Christians and I am blessed to have met 100 more of them, and I am sure there might be more of us out there. I just do not get to do the Washington D.C. circuit as much as I would like to because now that I have five-year-old twins, most of my time is spent in being a mother. However, I feel if you go to church regularly, that is more than two times per year, then, you have a duty to vote and you have a right to vote for the Republican party. Why should a Christian vote for the Republican party? Well, first of all, as American citizens we have a right to vote and we should exercise that right. Do you know people were killed for us to get the privilege to vote? Think about that for a moment. Now, let me show you the Christian movement and the Republican party. When I joined as a member of the Republican party back in 2008, I just assumed that hey I am a lawyer and this is a natural progression of my career goals. I know I will join and become a politician, which after all is prestigious. But God had another plan for me; I was saved. I accepted Jesus in my life and I started to walk with God. God then showed me that being a lawyer and being into politics was his calling and not mine. God showed me that we must as Christians back the Republican agenda. Why? Because the Republican agenda is God's agenda. Here are just a few things as that we need to see as Christians. Please do not take my word for it, I want you to check your Bible. I want you to go back to your churches and share this book with your Pastor and tell him I told you that the Republican party has the Christian agenda and we as Christians and evangelists must now stand up and stand tall with the Republican party. Here are the reasons, prophecies, family and work.

The Bible is the Word of God and it is real. We cannot add to the Bible and we cannot subtract from it. The Bible said we need to stand with Israel (NKJ Psalm 135:4). The Bible tells us the Jews are the chosen ones (NKJ Isiah 41:8). So, how can you as a born again Christian vote for any other President who will not back Israel? Come on. Really read the Bible and stop playing games. This is why Jesus isn't back for us as yet because we are so caught up in the secular system. We have become so narcissistic. We think earth is where it will all happen and this is far from the truth. Stop looking to fit in and just be who God called you to be. If you feel you love Jesus, then the only right thing to do is to vote for the Republican ticket because it is close or it has all of the Christian agenda. You do not see Evangelic Christians backing Democrats. There is a reason for that. They know that there is evil and there is good and the Democrats want to promote Satan's agenda. I said it. Other Christians know what I am talking about when they see the democrats living on Satan's agenda, for example, encouraging people to not work. Marry whoever you want!! Soon you might be able to marry your dog, just leave it to the democrats. We studied this in law school; it is called Beastiality. It is a crime now in America to sleep with your animal, but I have a feeling under the Democratic agenda, it will soon no longer be a crime to have sex with your dog, your cat, or your snake. Yes people, we need to draw morality in the sand somewhere and the Democrats are afraid of doing that. They just want to be the party of all inclusion and the Republicans, their mother and father, will come to straighten them out. This is how it is. There is good in this world but there is bad too. The Democrats are bad and the only reason the Democrats get away with so much is because of the good the Republicans do when they come into office and reign in the badness and madness of the Democratic party. That way the world is a bit balanced. But let's look at Israel. If you are Christian, you know Jesus is coming back to Israel. He didn't say he might, He said he will. The Bible said God is not a man where he would lie. So why would you back a President that isn't going to back Israel? How much faith do you have? Why can't you as a Christian take a stand? Do you think it is easy for me to write this book and broadcast to the world that I have Jesus. Do you think I won't be getting a backlash from this? I am a trial lawyer okay? I have a secular job and I intermingle every day with secular people. They have no idea that I attend church every Sunday. Now I am telling the world to love Jesus and to back the President of the United States for November 2020 because he has the Christian agenda. But why am I doing this? I am doing this because I must honor God. I am no longer going to stay back and look puzzled on how life should unfold. I am going to encourage blacks, Christians, and just about any voter to get out of their comfort zone and come November 2020, vote for the

Republican party and President Donald J. Trump. Do you want to usher in Jesus? If your answer is yes, then back a President that loves Israel—that is Trump. Trump is the only President who had the guts to move the United States Embassy to Jerusalem, which is biblical. That is prophecy coming to play. Do you see how we as Christians can move this world? We have no idea how powerful we are when we work together. As Christians our pay isn't on earth, it is in heaven. All we need to do as Christians if we are called to be in government is move the Republican party and the Christian agenda. I do not have a problem with Muslims either, and you as a Christian should not have a problem with them too. You need to love everyone. Do you know that the Muslims are a part of Abraham's family? Just read the Bible. Abraham had two kid, Ismael and Isaac. Isaac was the promised child and that is where the Jewish religion came from. Ismael was Abraham's son and God made a promise that Ismael's descendants would always be okay (Genesis 15:18 (NIV). This explains why God has given the Arab World Oil. Yes! God is the one blessing the Muslims. Muslims are not the devil. I know Christians who think Muslims are the devil. In fact, Muslims are a part of God's plan. If they weren't, then they would not have been on earth. There is a reason Israel is next to Iran and surrounded by all those Muslim nations. This is what God wanted. I know pastors won't agree with me but I just got back from London, England and I can tell you the Arabs are very blessed in London. This is what God wants for them. It is God's will that the Arabs have oil and for us to work with the Muslims. Of course, then there are terrorist, but that is less than 10% of the Muslim population and that portion is all Devil. Trust me, in due time, God will save the Muslims. As Christians, our job is to love them. We should not judge Muslims even if they walk by just showing their eyes. We need to figure a way to minister to them. We cannot reach the people we judge. So please, Christians do not let the simple things divide us. That is not our job. Our job as Christians on earth is not to criticize others; our job is to get the truth to people and spread love. One way we Christians can do this is by hijacking the Republican party to can get our message going.

In fact, God is the one blessing every single nation. So, how can you hate the Muslims if they are all God's people, but this will be for another story. Understand there is a fundamental difference between Muslims and extreme terrorists. You might never meet a terrorist, so stop thinking that every Muslim is a terrorist because they are not! Let your government fight the terrorist, and our jobs as Christians and people is to love everyone who comes into this country. The Republican party needs to do more to get the Muslims on board. I will write another book to follow through on that, but I think there will be a day when the Muslim nations will be open to hearing the Word of God. So, as Christians, we need to see that momentum coming.

Chapter 11

MUCH TO DO ABOUT RUSSIA.

This might be the biggest reason to come out and vote for Trump come November 2020. The Democrats created this untruthful story of Trump being helped by the Russians to win the election in November 2016. Now looking back, I always believed Trump would be vindicated. It is clear to me and now to the rest of the world and the entire voting block that Trump didn't collide with the Russians in interfering with the election. Don't take my word for it. Read what Robert Muller who was a special prosecutor had to say about it. The Russian meddling was much to do about anything. The democrats know that Trump is a strong leader and that he will be elected come November 2020. So, rather than having the focus on the good President Trump is doing to the economy, they believe in creating crap to make people think that President Trump cannot win the election by himself. The Russian meddling was a big nothing burger. Have you ever eaten a burger that has been hyped so much but then when you bite into it, it was nothing? It didn't taste as good as the other burgers, but you bought it anyway because the burger was hyped up; this is the same for the Russian meddling.

DEMOCRATS ARE SORE LOSERS.

What it boils down to is sore losers. The Democrats had Mr. Trump and the GOP a landslide the election and come 2018, the

Democrats will have more seats to defend than the GOP. With Mr. Donald Trump being a good campaigner and the possibility of getting the vote out, the Democrats really have no cards to play at this time. So why not just create a distraction this early in the year? That way Mr. Trump's polls will just slip and fall and then the GOP will be left with very little options. The GOP, in turn, will not want to campaign with Mr. Trump. As such, the GOP will not have much power movement behind them and the Democrats will have a strong hope of winning the 2020 elections and taking the senator over. Really, this Russian meddling thing is fake news just as the birther movement thing was on President Obama. Remember, people use to say that President Obama was born in Kenya and Mr. Obama had to produce his birth certificate to show he was indeed born in America; he was born in Hawaii. The shoes have now fallen on the GOP's foot. The Democratic party and the Liberal media are trying very hard to undermine Mr. Trump. That way, the Democratic party will garnish power. Since Mr. Trump has never held public office, the only thing that the Democrats can find to create a distraction or an illusion is that Russia has been meddling into the election and the Trump campaign knew about it or requested help from the Russians.

JARED KUSHNER AND THE BACK CHANNEL TO RUSSIA

So here is what we know. Someone's email from the DNC was hacked. The IP address showed that it came from Russia. The Trump transition team have very little experience in government and so Mr. Trump's son-in-law Jared Kushner reached out to the Russians to set up a backchannel to get through to the Kremlins. Have you ever called your doctor's office? You are not getting the back numbers for him? However, let us say you are a doctor and you are trying to reach another doctor to discuss a file. You are provided with another number. It is just like your work. Let us say you are a supervisor at your job and have over 5000 emails and phone calls per hour. Your wife or husband wants to reach you just to check in to see how things are going. They probably either have your personal cell phone number and email address that is a direct contact to you; this is what a backchannel is. When you are a part of the government, you have to be able to reach other governments really fast and not in the way I would reach out to the government. The Liberal media and the Democrats are making this backchannel statement bigger than it really is. The only reason it looks so strange to many is that Mr. Trump hired many people with little or no political experience causing them to start from the ground up. Mr. Kushner had to build his contacts from the ground up, and so, it looks bigger than it is. Let me tell you something. The majority of people in Congress are lawyers. Lawyers are storytellers. Lawyers are trained to make an inference from anything. Lawyers cannot stop being lawyers! Though they changed their jobs and are no longer in Washington DC, their lawyer skills are still hard at work. So now, they just make these stories up by just using inference. Backchannels must equate to corruption. Unfortunately, what these Democrats are doing is slowing down the progress of changes for the American people by distracting and taking precious time away from the Trump administration. By doing that, the Democrats will come off in 2020 and say that Mr. Trump did not accomplish anything, when, in fact, the real losers are the voters because Mr. Trump truly wants to make America great again and we need to provide Mr. Trump with the tools and the focus he needs to get this done. As time goes by, we are going to see that Mr. Kushner did nothing wrong and that setting up a backchannel was pretty standard. With very little experience in government, Mr. Kushner must have done what he felt he could to get a backchannel for the government, and that government happened to be Russia. Okay, so what? Big deal. We need to talk to our enemies as well as our friends. We live in one world and we have to know what is going on. The Russian conspiracy is just as bad as the birthers' movement. It is time for the Democrats to start focusing on what the American people sent them (Democrats) to Washington D.C. to do, which is to create jobs and promote health and welfare of this great nation. The Democrats are too slick. They know in 2020, they (Democrats) will have a lot of seats to defend and they know the GOP will have a good chance of sweeping victory with President Donald J. Trump in office. So why not just smear the President and the White House? That way, they (Democrats) can get ahead. In the end, none of this crap matters any more. Robert Muller, the Chief Prosecutor for the Russian Meddling, has now made it clear that he will not be moving forward in prosecuting Trump because there was no intermeddling on Trump's part. In order to have collusion, Trump should have known about it. It cannot be that the Russians tried to help. I mean, I am trying to help Trump win the Election November 2020, but does that mean I am in collusion with Trump? No, it doesn't. Please do not let this little political swing and political madness about the Russians interfering with the election get you down. You have a great President and you need to keep him in office. Trump will not be impeached. This is the only buzz words the Democrats want to use into scaring us so that we do not vote for Trump. Do not buy into the Democratic hype; rather get out and go vote to elect perhaps the greatest President of the United States of America of our generation and history. Go out and vote to re-elect Donald J. Trump for President of the United States of America come November 2020. With these words, I part for now. Remember, God bless America. God bless the President of the United States, Donald J. Trump. God bless you, Mr. President. We as the American people look forward to having you for four more years to run our wonderful country. It is an honor and a privilege to write this book. It is a blessing to live in the greatest nation in the world. Everyone until another time. Take care. Go out and vote Trump. Vote in droves. Vote for the Republican party come November 2020.

CHAPTER 12

Trump's Win & The Right to Bear Arms In America

I remember when I came to this country at around 19 years old. I didn't know Jesus. I was desolate and one day a friend took me to a church in Margate, Florida called Abundant Life Christian Church. I found Jesus. I became born again. And I have not look backed on that old ragged secular life every since. Mark you. I do have sins (who doesn't). I have slipped and fall. But the Lord has been good to me to pick me up and I just get back up. I quickly started reading my bible and embraced the christian cause. I started to believe that abortions were sins. Because a baby who is unborn is just alive and well as a person like you and me. So why should a woman kill a baby and then label it as abortion? You know research also prove that most if not all the women who commit abortions went on to feel depress later in life. This is because of guilt. These women know that abortion is a sin and a crime. But this secular world we live in label it as something else. Abortion is a crime and a sin. And someday the American voters will rule against this ugly sin. Unborn has the right to live. The way you and I have a right to live. We are all creators of God. God made us and give us life. The unborn deserve to live and not die. But back to what I wanted to say. Sorry, I get choked up when I think of abortion. I know it affects a lot of black people and I hope that blacks will see it for what it really is. It is a way for the culture to control blacks by reducing the population by having people do abortions. But as a christian, this has got to be something that you feel compel about. With this in mind, when i was aware that I was born again and I started to dive into politics- The first things my black friends told me is that I needed to be a democrat. of course, I had to ask why? And the answer was simple. Because you are black you needed to be a democrat. I was like, " but I am born again," shouldn't I side more with the republican party because it had more conservative values that the church held. And my black friends, just laugh me to scorn. My black friends just said, :look, don't ask any questions. You are a democrat okay. The democrats look out for the blacks. Forget the unborn. Worry more about the color of your skin. This didn't sit well with me. I felt that if I loved Jesus. If I loved the lord. I need to love the unborn and I need to hang close to the conservative values. And while, I won't be popular siding with the republican party, I had to become a republican because my faith in God won't allow me otherwise. And there you have the birth of a black christian evangelist. Of course, the media doesn't mention much about black christian evangelist because there aren't much black christian evangelist. Why is that? Because blacks are brain washed to become democrats whether they love the lord or not. Blacks are taken for granted. The democrats just steal black people's voice. The democrats steal black people vote. The democrats just steal black people right. And that is just how it goes. But a decent amount of evangelist, particularly the White christian conservative voted for President Trump. And years after years, people are just fascinating with the big issue - Why do White Christian Evangelist vote for President Trump?

We are about to find out.

Evangelist tend to back the Republican party in historical numbers. "According to 2004 exit polls, George W. Bush won 78 percent of their votes; in 2008, John McCain won 74 percent; and in 2012, Mitt Romney won 78 percent."[1]

---

1   https://www.washingtonpost.com/news/monkey-cage/wp/2016/10/03/evangelical-voters-will-almost-surely-vote-for-donald-trump-heres-why/?utm_term=.834e1e721b02

Even before the Presidential election in November 2016, writers like Paul Goren and Christopher Chapp, of the Washington Post predicted that evangelist would vote for President Trump.[2] According to the Washington Post: "...our new research suggests that evangelical voters' views of Trump probably have much less to do with him (Trump) personally than with his (Trump) rhetoric on abortion and his promises to protect Christianity in America."[3] (emphasis added).

Here is what Franklin Graham, son of famous evangelist preacher, Billy Graham, had to say about the decision that many evangelist support President Trump for election:" "This election is about the Supreme Court and the justices that the next president will nominate," Graham said in a statement this weekend. "Evangelicals are going to have to decide which candidate they trust to nominate men and women to the court who will defend the constitution and support religious freedoms."[4]

NEVER HILLARY CLINTON OR ANY DEMOCRATIC CANDIDATE FOR PRESIDENT.

Another big issue why man evangelist voted for Trump had more to do with the fact that these evangelist would never see themselves voting for President Trump opponent- Ms. Hillary Clinton. Whether you are a democrat, a republican, a christian conservative, a liberal sector, Mrs. Clinton rubbed a lot of people the wrong way. Mrs. Clinton was a hard sell for the democratic party. If Mrs. Clinton could barely rally her own base, how

2   https://www.washingtonpost.com/news/monkey-cage/wp/2016/10/03/evangelical-voters-will-almost-surely-vote-for-donald-trump-heres-why/?utm_term=.834e1e721b02

3   https://www.washingtonpost.com/news/monkey-cage/wp/2016/10/03/evangelical-voters-will-almost-surely-vote-for-donald-trump-heres-why/?utm_term=.834e1e721b02

4   http://www.nbcnews.com/politics/2016-election/what-s-behind-evangelical-support-donald-trump-less-you-think-n666146

would she rally the evangelist voters who were always local for 3 decades to the republican party? This was a hard pill for many people to swallow. Mrs. Clinton was just not presidential enough for her own party, let alone the country. And while President Trump has been married 3 times, forgiveness is a big part of being a christian. Of course, "he who has no sin should cast the first stone." People are not expecting a perfect President as the only perfection to come is in Christ. The only perfection to come is Christ second coming. The only perfection to come is your faith in God. People didn't vote for a saint. People voted for a President. If you want a saint, then follow Christ. The world is full of sinners and even our Presidents and our dignities are not perfect. We are living in a fallen world. But the bible does say that God appoints our leaders. So if God appoints our leaders, then as men and women of God, let us pray and uplift our leaders. Let us show our leaders that Christ is the truth and the way. Let us stand up for our leaders.

President Trump promised to provide the evangelist voters with ultra conservative supreme court justices and for a better protection for christian evangelists. We are even beginning to see the promises being kept by President Donald Trump. President Trump added a conservative justice to the Supreme Court; Neil Gorsuch. And President Trump is looking to do away with some of the harsh political issues that Christians face. Here is a dump one for you. A church can lose its 501 C if a church leader or someone invited by the church speaks or endorses a political candidate.[5]   This Johnson amendment were pastors are not free to endorse a political candidate from the pulpit or the entire church loses its tax code is baloney (and not the sandwich).

5   Trump has promised to repeal the so-called Johnson Amendment, a 1954 provision that prohibits tax-exempt organizations from participating in political activities. Proposed by then-Senator Lyndon B. Johnson and later revised by Congress, it keeps churches and other non-profits from lobbying for specific causes, campaigning on behalf of politicians, and supporting or opposing candidates for…. https://www.theatlantic.com/politics/archive/2016/08/how-trump-is-trying-to-put-more-money-in-politics/493823/

Come on. We live in a modern and competitive world a lot of christians rely upon the church to make simple decisions as to whether I should have kids, what job must I have. Why can't we rely upon the church on who to vote for? Many christians don't have time to join political establishment and so these christians rely upon the church to provide a quick summary on what each candidate stands for. It is only fair and just that Pastors be allowed to endorse political candidates who will further the christian movement and Israel.

TRUMP AND THE ECONOMY

Nothing feels more like defeat, that not having a penny to your name. Nothing spells defeat like not having a job to your name. Nothing sells defeat like feeling hopeless about your financial future. And this my friend. This my dear American brothers and sisters in christ and outside of Christ is why we need a President like Mr. Trump. President Trump is a symbol of American wealth. President Trump reaps the havoc of the American dream. President Trump understands what it takes to build wealth literally from the ground up.   President Trump has not even been in office for over one year in the White House. and what can you see with the American economy? I will name a few. Jobs, Jobs, and more Jobs. Every day, we wake up to hear more jobs are being created, right here in America. The unemployment is at an all time low. The stock market is at an all time high.[6] The future looks hopeful. The real estate market is on a uptick. Business are again investing in infrastructures in America. Apple promised to create more jobs in America. other Manufactories are bringing plants to and back to America. Other manufactures

---

6   The S&P 500 is up more than 12 percent since Election Day, unemployment has reached a 16-year low and economic growth in the coming year is expected to reach 2.3 percent, more robust growth than the 1.6 percent it grew in 2016. http://thehill.com/policy/finance/337203-economy-emerges-as-bright-spot-for-trump

are leaving plants in America. Manufactories are deciding not to take their jobs overseas, to places like Mexico. Instead, Manufactories want to build infrastructure here in America. Don't you are just proud to be an American? Isn't this a wonderful time for us? Isn't this President really making us feel good again? is this President making us feel great again? Isn't this President making America great again?

I have the pleasure of spending time in New York. Manhattan. Manhattan, oh boy is truly a city. New York is probably the greatest or one of the greatest city in the World. And this is where President Trump made his name and his millions. Opps, I mean his billions. In the heart of the greatest city, manhattan. What can I tell you about Manhattan? Well, Manhattan is home to many millionaires and billionaires. I am sure you have heard the saying before. If you want to be rich, then live where the millionaire live. Visit the cities where the millionaires flock to. If you want to rich, then live where the millionaires and billionaires are living? Why? As humans, we adapt. Life is about survival. You become who and what you associate yourself with. You become who and what you obsess about the most. What am i saying? I am saying that wealth has surround New York City for decades. President Trump is the ultimate symbol of wealth. When you think of wealth and success, you think of President Trump. Now, Mr. Trump is our President, don't you think we have a chance of getting a healthy economy because America is now being run by a President who lived, breath and think wealth most of his life? People strive in the environment they are most comfortable with. President Trump is all about the money. I am sure you have watched or read the news about President Trump and the wealth he accumulated prior to entering in the White house. This just shows you that wealth is on Mr. Trump's mind, day and night and some of that wealth and the thinking of wealth will be shifted to us- the American people.

The Economy, the America Dream.

I love to relate to people. Because it makes me feel real. And I love writing books, articles and talking on radio and meeting my clients by phone, or Skype or at my office in Boca Raton, Florida. It gives me a feeling of realness. I am not telling you any story to brag because it doesn't matter how pretty, thin, successful or happy you are. There is always someone who can outdo you in terms of looks, money, success and happiness. But I would be lying if I didn't say that President Trump has been an inspiration for me and my sister (who happens to be an Pilot for a major US Carrier) for years. You see, when I was 19 years old. I was poor. I left my parent's house with one suitcase to my name. That was all the possession I had. I struggled like most 19 years old do. I went to bed at times with no food in my stomach. Being 19 with no food in stomach, was okay at the time. I survived. I remembered wanting to be rich or free from debt and stress. And I read one of President's Trump book, "The Art of the Deal." From reading President Trump's book, I felt motivated that things can turn around for me. I read other books written by other financial gurus and real estate gurus. Well, I am here to tell you that nearly 20 years now, and I no longer go to bed hungry. My partner and I enjoy a privilege life raising 3.5 year old twins. I have had the pleasure of hosting my own radio show, being guests on national radio and tv show and living in my eyes the America dream. I feel like some of this has to do with just reading books like what President Trump wrote about. President Trump gives us hope that our finances can turn around. Now, I just read an article that is saying exactly what I am saying. Why do you think the stock market is doing so well, while in the first 120 days while President Trump just got to offie? As of August 2017, President Trump hasn't passed any tax or any business regulation or law for people to be pumped up. Wall street is pumped up. Business are taking risk and either building plants in America or leaving jobs in America. But Wall street and other investors understand that any regulation that passes with business and any tax reform will benefit the economy because that really is all President Trump understands. President Trump is and was a very successful business man. And as such, when President Trump goes to pass business regulations and tax reform, it is going to benefit the economy. That means all of us here in America.[7]

I consider writing books as a way to get the message directly to the American people. I am just like you. I am living in America. I have children that I need to raise. I get up every morning and I work. I have two special need kids. I have more to do than most people with typical or healthy children. I have to plan for dinner for my kids. I have to travel at times away from home for business. I worry about my children and their future. I have a college plan set up for my kids. I hope the best for my children. I worry about their future and what life will be like for my children when I am dead. I wonder what my grandchildren will be like in this country if and every I get grandchildren. I believe that the liberal media play mind games with us because it has other motives. Please do not follow what you hear and see on television every day. We need to do what is right for ourselves and the children and grandchildren that we will have or already have. Don't be fooled. President Trump is going to make the economy great. It will be President Trumps' priority to take care of America. So get out in drove and vote for President Trump and support President Trump and all his agenda.

---

7   Trump ran as a businessman who would enact economic policies that would benefit the private sector, and the stock market has been driven up on the idea that regulatory reform and huge tax cuts are coming. If they fail to materialize, it's possible those gains could roll back. http://thehill.com/policy/finance/337203-economy-emerges-as-bright-spot-for-trump

5 Reasons President Trump is good for the economy.

I am writing this book because I have one feeling. I need to share the truth with others. I am gifted with the ability to write. I have the ability to do research and I feel like this is the easiest way to share the truth with the American people. We are so blessed these days that we can get our message out through social media, and books. We can by-pass all of the other ways people get news and just get it to people in short snaps. These are the reasons, we need to feel good about our President and these are the reasons we will need to come out in 2018, 2020 and 2022 and vote for the republican party and re-elect President Trump. Here are the 5 reasons President Trump will be good for the economy.

1. President Trump is a billionaire.

President Trump never made his money from politics. President Trump went to the White house as a very wealthy man. Because President Trump is attracted to wealth, all President Trump will do is bring wealth to the America people.

2. We are already seeing the savings with President Trump.

Okay, so this might not be a big thing to you. But think about the fact that President Trump saves us millions of dollars for Air Force One. I am sure you have heard that Air Force one needs to be renovated or we need to get a new one. President Trump didn't like the price tag on what it would cost the American people and so President Trump renegotiated for a new price. It will save us millions if not billions of dollars.

3. NAFA IS BEING RENEGOTIATED.

Again, President Trump talks about the unfair trade with Canada and Mexico. It cost tax payers millions per year. Because of President Trump, Americans will save a ton of money because President Trump will renegotiated with NAFTA.

4. PRESIDENT TRUMP IS GETTING THE EU TO PAY ITS FAIR SHARE.

Again, these things might seem minor to you. But if you are ever one a budget. If you ever want to save money. You have to look at where all the money is going. Forget going for a raise. First, you have to cut the dead weight, or the dead fact. You have to rein in the spending. And President Trump understands that. Let's say you spend $9.00 per day on cigarette and $6.00 per day on coffee. If you ever go on a budget, you will write down just how much that cigarette is costing you per day. Then you will calculate how much it is costing you per month. And then you will look to see how much it is costing you per year and how much the coffee is costing you per day Then you will look at just how much the coffee is costing you per month. And then you will look at just how much the coffee is costing you per year. And you will start cutting back on those purchases. By cutting back on those purchases, you will have more money saved. And that is exactly what President Trump has been doing. President Trump sees that the EU, many nations are not putting their fair share into the pot. And that isn't fair because it is costing the American taxpayer more money. And do you know from President Trump speaking up, many nations are now paying more. It was just a simple talk. But every little adds up. And again, you only will know that if you ever try to cut back on debt.

5. THE STOCK MARKET IS UP.

These are just a few examples. I could give you more. But because of President Trump, the stock market is up. of course, President Trump hasn't done anything yet to make the market go uptick. But it is future prediction. Wall Street understands no matter what happens in the next 4 years, the economy will be strong because President Trump is all about money and because President Trump is all about money, the economy is going to be stronger. People are confident in a President like President Trump because money is what President Trump understands. And I know people will say, oh come on, President Trump has put his companies into bankruptcy. But these are people who do not understand the bankruptcy laws and how America is. Of course, if you can put your company in bankruptcy to get some type of leverage, then why not do it. President Trump is not the only rich person in America to use the bankruptcy system to get leverage. We see it every day with fortune 500 companies. These companies file for bankruptcy protection to either get out of a judgment or to renegotiate with others. So why is it okay for those fortune 500 companies to do it? But President Trump doing it, it is wrong. During the recession in 2008, I watched all these wealthy business men file bankruptcy to get out of millions of debt. And then within 5 years, they bounce back with nothing but wealth. Smart business men and women in America has constantly use the bankruptcy system to get out of excessive debt and to restructure and start over. Personally, I do not see anything wrong with it. And if you are Christian, don't tell me it is wrong. Please read the bible and read the book of Deuteronomy. In the bible, God said that every 7 years debt is suppose to be wiped out. We are only suppose to have debt for 7 years and then we need to get it wiped out. Since our greedy creditors won't let us go when we are in debt, the recession and the bankruptcy code, will do that for us. So there is nothing wrong in getting forgiven or let go of your debt. Of course, there is a problem if you are doing it through fraud or if you are abusing the bankruptcy system or taking advantage of your creditors by going into debt purposely with the intention of not paying back your creditors. That will be a problem .But the way the bankruptcy code is set up, it will be hard to game the system. So have an open mind. Getting rid of debt through bankruptcy is not a crime. And it is not a sin.

Chapter 13

Why We Must Vote To Re-Elect President Donald J. Trump Come November 2020

I know most people think that Washington DC is too far and too remote from us to really have any impact. Really, Let me count thy ways.

Health care any one?

Do you remember when we could pick and choose what we wanted and whether we wanted to be insured? Now think of Obamacare. You might not have met President Obama, but today, his failing signature healthcare is now a part of every day life. If you never cared about Washington, you better start caring. Washington D.C. has the power to prick your finger, literally. Some people are paying over $800.00 per month for a mandatory health care President Obama brought into law. And Obamacare is failing and God knows what is going to happen aside from we will keep paying a fortune to be insured until something else comes to play. So when you think your vote doesn't count, think again. The days of not caring about politics are now over. Let me remind you of other issues. I hate to be the bearer of bad news. But you live in this world and this country like I do. And I don't care where in America you are, Washington D. C. has the power to impact us all.

Legal and illegal Immigrants

Remember, how many people laughed off the fact that President Trump was running for President of the United States. What did President Trump say, " Build that Wall." and most people laughed saying, there is no way President Trump will build a wall. Immigration anyone? we are going to be tuff on immigration. And most people say, just ignore President Trump, he President Trump said he be tuff on immigrants. Global warming is a hoax. Let's just ignore President Trump, he won't be president anyway. Well, how is that going for you now? You care about immigration, well, you never took President Trump serious and now you will have to deal with the consequences on whether President Trump build that wall. And whether President Trump reduce legal immigrants and wipe out illegal immigrants. All because we, including myself, just figure that Washington D.C. is too far away from us. And nothing that gets pass in Washington D.C. will really affect my life. Well, I hope this is the last election that you plan on ignoring. Because Washington D.C has the power to make your life a living hell.

Global Warming, Global Warning anyone

Again, all I can recall is people just saying, President Trump is just saying things because it sounds good. Well, let me know how it is going now. Whether we like it or not, President Trump has and had the power to remove us from the Paris Climate agreement and in deed, President Trump removed us. Of course, most people do not like this. Because scientists are saying that Global warming is real and not a hoax. But you know what. Again, Washington D.C has no power over us. Please let me know how that is going when you get a lot warmer as the years go by. I just feel like if you care about anything, you need to care what is going on in Washington D.C. and I am not saying you have to be a political guru and become a lobbyist or quit your day job and move your family to Washington D.C to get involved into politics. You can get involved at a local level. You can get involve by just making phone calls and writing letters and paying attention and of course, voting. You can get involve by encouraging others to vote. Because that is what brings real changes, the ability to vote and make a difference.

THE UNITED STATES OF AMERICA ECONOMY

Under President Obama, we lived in a major recession, and most of us live in a major depression. The democratic party and President Obama had no way of stimulating the economy and millions of Americans ended up losing their homes, losing their jobs, and losing their savings. Again this is what Washington D. C does. It really mirrors the leader. Now that President Trump is in power, the economy is getting better. We have the lowest unemployment rate in decades. and the stock market is going up. The U.S. dollar is strong. In fact, I got to the post office a lot because I am an attorney and I am constantly mailing documents on behalf of my clients. And I need those documents to be tracked. I noticed that in the last year, many people are applying for their U.S Passport. Why is that? Because the U.S. Dollar is so strong that many Americans can again enjoy a decent trip to Europe. Americans are feeling confident in their ability to go overseas, and spend money. We have President Trump to thank for this.

THE SUPREME COURT OF THE UNITED STATES.

"Federal government keep your hands off my body." This is what most people are saying. But you know what, these people still didn't give a darn and these people didn't vote. Now President Trump has the ability to nominate judges in all the Federal Court. (whenever a vacancy comes up) Do not complain when you get conservative judges who interpret the constitution the way it should be. After all, you didn't even bother to vote. And these federal judges will determine the law of the land .Of course, if you violate the law of the land, you will be punished. And you had the ability to shape the future by casting your vote, but you didn't bother. So please, do not complain. "Federal Government, I guess you can put your hands on my body, because I neglect to vote."

EDUCATION AND STUDENT LOANS.

Again, the people who didn't vote are now complaining because President Trump nominated Betsy DeVos to be Education Secretary. I know you have or know someone who has student loans. This will be affected. And Affirmative action will be affected too. Yes. Ms. DeVos has the power to get rid of affirmative action. But again, let me talk the way the non voters talk" Washington D.C is too far away for us to care." Let me know how that is going for you. Because I could literally dedicate an entire book on how Washington D. C. affect our lives, how Washington D.C. affect your life. But this is something you should have already know. But in case you didn't, I am just summarizing a few things that are at steak here. And yes, I am for the republican Party and President Trump. But I am mostly for people's ability to get involved in elections. This is why I am writing this book. I am trying to get you excited about being part of the big changes in America. and I am trying to show you how your one vote, is making a difference in today's life.

Tax Reform

There are two things that are certain in life- death and taxes. And since you will face both, why not vote for a President that will reform the tax code. This is another thing you can relate to. Because you have to pay taxes, or you know of someone who has to pay taxes that you care deeply for. The less taxes you pay, the more money goes into your pocket. That equates to an instant raise, and instant savings for you. That means, more money for you to spend or save for your family. Do not follow the democrats who tell you the more you pay, is the more we can help the poor. This is all bull crap. First of all, the government should not be taking care of the poor. The church and charity should be taken care of the poor. Do you see the mess we are in today with all this wasteful spending with the government. I meet poor people all the time, through my line of work and they are able body. but they refuse to work because they want the government to give them money. Do you blame them? Why work, when you can live for free. Of course, not working will affect your morales. But since people figure a way to game the system and get free money from the government , why would they need to work? of course, for you and me, making 250.00 per week from the government doesn't seem like money. And getting food stamp is not the idea American life style. But for lazy people and people who know that the government would pay it, do you blame them from going on the system? Do not be fooled by Senator Elizabeth Warren and Senator Bernie Sanders who believe that the government should keep getting fatter and we should be come a socialist country. You won't like it. Just go to Europe for a visit and tell me if you do not think those people there are miserable. When the government give you money the government eventually will control you. The government will start thinking for you. Do you know why the government wants to give you money? Because a bunch of lawyers in Washington D.C. who call themselves politicians want to have a job for the rest of their lives. And so they will give you money in exchange you will continue to vote for them. Do you think that Senator Bernie Sanders and Senator Elizabeth Warren live the way those on welfare live? no they do not. These politicians are living high on the hog. These democratic senators are eating at 5 star restaurants, where they serve foie gros and aged to perfect the ultimate filet mignon. Thees democratic senators are taking 5 star vacations to destination that the rich, and famous jet to. Perhaps places like Maldives Hawaii and Seychelles. Of course, your welfare check cannot get you into the 5 star restaurants or the fancy vacations of these democratic politicians go to. You are just a pawn to the democratic party. "lean me your ear, and I will pollute your mind." "Lend me your ear, and i will control your mind." This is exactly the motto the democratic party should adopt. Why am I so passionate about this? Because I am a black woman living in this country. And I know that the only way blacks feel and stay poor is because of the politicians that we have entrusted to get us ahead. This is why I refuse to be a democratic. It is all a trick. The democrats want to enslave the black man and the black woman, by keeping us ignorant of what hard work can truly do. The democrats are trying to poison the minds of able body blacks and other poor into thinking that welfare is the only way we are going to survive. Well, I have news for you. We are done with your scam. Democrats, it is time you let the people go. it is time you let go of the blacks and the poor. And let us know that there is a president, in the White House, name President Trump who is about to look out for the poor, the rich, the black, the white, the educated and the uneducated. So get your hands, Mr Democrat off my wallet.

THE HOUSING MARKET

From my picture, you should be able to tell that I am black. It is not common for a black person to be a republican And so because of this, I have to get lectured by my family members who are all democrats. yes they are black and so they are democrats. My sister and her husband have to pay for the wedding of my niece. Now my sister and her husband are hard workers. But like you and many other people, money is tight. So what do you think my sister and her husband will do, work a second job. This time in the area of real estate. Why is this possible? Simple because President Trump is now in office. Because of President Trumps banks are feeling confident again to loan money. And people are feeling confident to buy homes. If if wasn't for President Trump I do not think my sister and her husband would be able to pay for my niece wedding. You see back when President Obama was in office, the housing market was a disaster. I am sure you have heard of the Dodd-Frank Act. It makes it nearly impossible for banks to loan money. of course, banks should be regulated. But it should never come to the point where there are so much regulations that lending has become impossible. I hate banks. I sue banks for a living. I don't believe that banks are fair. However, banks are in the business of loaning money and the consumers and the borrowers are in the business of borrowing money. Let the consumer and the banks figure things out. Why would the government step in? the Government has made so much regulations that it makes no sense. Really. I am a licensed realtor in the State of Florida. And recently I was closing on a deal for a client. The purchase price was around $250,000.00. Because of the Dodd-frank rule, a random appraisal was selected to appraise the property? why? Because some wise lawyer in Washington D.C who has never sold real estate made a law that says, in order for the appraising system not be rigged, let us give random appraisal the properties to appraisal. And guess what? We then end up with an inexperience appraisal who has no idea what things in that area appraisal for and the appraisal provides a very low value. What if you were told you needed to get a surgery done, because you have some type of stomach issue. Would you like to get some random doctor that you have never heard of do the surgery on you? Your answer is probably no. Of course not. Well, that is what the housing market is like now. Random appraisals that perhaps appraisal in rural areas, are now appraising properties in urban areas. Then the appraisal comes in really low and then when you try to dispute it, good luck. That is another red tape, enough to make you throw your hand up and walk away. Selling real estate and getting a mortgage are already stressful on its own. Now, re-altors and mortgage brokers have to deal with Washington DC, Dodd-Frank which is a nightmare all and in its self. If I wasn't hopeful that President Trump is going to make things better, I would have easily have left the real estate market. Trust me when I tell you rolling back the Dodd-Frank will be a good thing for borrowers. This will be a loss for the democratic party because of course, Senator Elizabeth Warren and Senator Bernie Sanders would like to propose socialism to America. By having the Dodd-Frank in place, the democrats are hoping to cripple the banking industry. That way, people cannot borrow money and people will be forced to live on welfare. Because face it, if you are a business owner and you would like to borrow against your home, if it be-comes impossible, you will eventually lose your drive and at some point, the government hand out will be growing and we will be like a socialist nation and *walla,* the government will explode. But this won't happen under President Trumps' watch. Thank God. The Dodd frank must be repel and it must be repeal now.

Chapter 14

Trump Must Win To Stop Socialism From Coming To America

Socialism versus Capitalism.

I love Europe. I go there a lot. In fact, I am taking my 3.5 year old twins along with my partner in September 2017. We went. So when I wrote this, we didn't go. But I took my kids to London and Amsterdam. I love to visit Europe. It is beautiful. But it is just not America. Many people are fascinated with Europe. After all, Europeans get 6 weeks of paid vacation minimum. But Europe is smaller than America. And Europe, most of it, is a socialist country. So what is at steak here in America? Well one thing that is at steak is capitalism. You see President Trump will keep capitalism alive and well. Yes people. America is based upon capitalism and those who do not like it, well they can leave. Those of us who like capitalism voted for President Trump. Why? Because we want to be able to create wealth. We want to be able to create work. We want to be able to create freedom. And President Trump is your man. Look, this is my word to you. If you like capitalism, then vote for President Trump and the republican party. If you like socialism, then do yourself and the rest of us a favor, move to Europe or Venezuela and embrace their ideology. and it why allow you to pen letters, then drop me a line. Let me know how it is going for you. Let me know how it feels to be free. If you like communism, which some people love Mayor Bill DeBasio, then move to Cuba or North Korea. Drop me a line while you re there as well. Let me know how its s going. This is like an al la carte menu here. If you want Chinese food you go to a Chinese restaurant. We don't have China coming to us. We go and get the Chinese food. If we want steak, we go to a steak restaurant. If we want fish, we go to a seafood restaurant. We do not go to a japans restaurant and insist to the chief to cook us Italian food because for some reason, it taste much better. Just like if we love sweet, we do not buy salt and then pour sweet on there, hoping it taste salty. So please. I am sick of these liberals who try to tell me that socialism should come here to America. America should be socialism to be fair to the poor and people should help the poor enjoy more life. Socialist tells me that America should be socialist because think of it this way, It is like buying a home, where it gets old and you just paint it. No. This is bigger than painting a home. This is saying a chair is now a car, because the chair has 4 legs and a car has 4 wheels. They must be the same. Its s not. American is a capitalism country. and it will never be social. Not today, not tomorrow and not forever more. If you want more for yourself, then embrace, President Trump and the republican party. If you capitalism, then vote for President Trump and the republican party. If you want freedom, then vote Republican and President Trump. President Trump and the republican represents freedom. As Martin Luther King once said, Let freedom reign. My word to you is let President Trump and the republican reign.

CAPITALISM HAS TO BE THE DOMINANT WEIGHT IN AMERICA. WE CANNOT AFFORD SOCIALISM.

a chair was built to sit on. A chair was not built to stand on. A chair was not built to be placed on your head as a decoration. What am I trying to say to you? America was built on capitalism. If the democratic party try to rebuild America on socialism, then

America will crash and burn. You cannot reinvent the wheel. A car was build to drive by sober people. This is why when people drive car at high speech the cars crash. This is why when people drive cars when they are drunk, they crash or worst, they kill someone. You cannot reinvent any wheel, no matter how smart you are. If you want a socialist country, it is best to go to a socialist country. The bible said ""And no one puts new wine into old wineskins. For the wine would burst the wineskins, and the wine and the skins would both be lost. New wine calls for new wineskin."[8] We are happy here in our capitalist country. Yes, it is not perfect. But we cannot get socialist here.

WE ALREADY HAVE SOME FORM OF SOCIALISM IN AMERICA ALREADY

I am not sure why Americans would like to experience a socialist country, when we already have some form of socialist products here in America. Most Americans have never traveled overseas. In fact, it is only 5% of the American population to hold a United States Passport. That tells me that many Americans have never been to Europe to even experience socialism. I bet most of these Americans who are talking about socialism do not even have friends or families that live in Europe to explain really what is going on over there. I love Europe. Do not get me wrong. I would love to buy a second home in Greece and spend some time there. But I do not think i would live in Europe over America. Even when America experience the great recession, America was still the best place on earth to live. And do not tell me it is because I am a lawyer and a realtor that things are going well to me. I do not consider myself to be rich. I am frugal. I shop at discounted stores so I can pay for stuff for my kids. I am a mother like most of you are. I have twins that turn 4 come November 2017. I have to pay for their health insurance. I have to pay for

---

8   Mark 2 versus 22, the new living version of the Bible.

their extra classes. I have to pay for their swimming classes. I have to buy them food and pay for child care for 2 kids. So I am not rich. Children require a lot of time and money. So I sacrifice for myself in order to make ends meet. I work two jobs and there is no shame in that. I do not shop at Macy's or Nordstrom or any high end store. On a Saturday, you can find me at T.J. Max or Walmart or Target. Yes. I am a lawyer shopping in these stores because they are practical for me. My money stretch more. And what about my yearly trips to Europe you might ask. I either purchased my tickets 60 days in advance (where they are cheap). Or I buy tickets or low carrier airlines like Wow air or Norwegian airlines. And where do I stay when I go to Europe. I do the Airbnb stuff because I can cook when I get there and I save money on cooking. At some point, I will write a book on frugality. This is what is missing from the American people. The idea of living frugal. If you live below your means, then you will not have any needs. But of course, we all want to keep up with the Jones, and for most Americans, we want to keep up with the Kardashians. I have no problem with the Kardashians. But their lifestyle is not mine. I love living frugal. Because the bible told me to owe no man nothing but love. Based upon a frugal live, you won't need to want to be socialist. You will live below your means, and you will have no lack. You should try the frugality sometimes. It is not as hard as you think it is. With amazon.com and eBay.com now, it is even easier than ever to live frugal.

And guess what? Those socialist forms in American are already broken. So before we dive into the broken socialist form of America, let's look at what those forms are: (1) Social Security and (2) Medicaid.

SOCIAL SECURITY

I am 41 year old writing this book and I hate to be the bearer of bad news. But social security will not be around for you and me when we retire. Ahh, don't say that. Yes, I have to stay it because it is the truth. Social security is like a socialist product that should work. But it doesn't. It doesn't work because social security is already bankrupted. The government is actually robbing from one generation to pay another. If you do not believe my word, then just read on line and other books on why social security is bankrupt. I wanted to bring this to your attention because I remembered when Senator Sanders was running, I had an American nanny who lived with me and cared for my kids while I go out and work. My American nanny who at the time was only 23 years old wanted Senator Sanders to win the election because after all, Senator Sanders promised a lot of socialist programs to the young people. Now, you might be saying, why would a United States born person do a live in job. The answer is simple. There were no other opportunities for my nanny. She couldn't complete college because the cost of college was too high and her parents like most of our parents were poor. Because of this, my American nanny only option was to do a live in job. I paid her a stipend and she lived in my house rent free while she cared for my kids. Of course, both my American nanny (let's call her Jane), and I would often talked about politics. If you have met you, you understand that I am passionate about the republican party and feel that everyone should be a republican. I felt Jane was lost and confused about the democratic party because the democratic party often target poor people and tell them (poor people) that live would be better once the democrats get elected. Well, we had a democratic president for the last 8 years, and please, poor people tell me how did you life get any better. It didn't. Anyway, back to Jane. Jane wanted Senator Sanders to win because Jane wanted a free education, a free house, and free health care. Jane felt that Senator Sanders would make everything better. I kept telling Jane that socialism doesn't work. and that Jane should go to Europe and tell me what she thinks. I think most Americans have never been to Europe and these Americans have no idea what socialism really is. I can tell you from a person who has the privilege of traveling overseas, Socialism really works. My partner and I just got back from Amsterdam and London and I noticed that while we were in Amsterdam, a very liberal and socialist nation, we paid for everything. Yes. I wanted to use the bathroom. And I went into a restaurant. I was not a patronize of the restaurant and guess what? I had to pay 50 cents to use the bathroom. Now, I traveled to Europe with a party of 5. Can you imagine if all 5 of us went to use the bathroom? That would have been 2.50 for 5 people. That is Euro by the way. So it would be around $3.50 in US dollars (depending on the conversion rate). I think that is a little expensive to use the bathroom, don't you think. I remember saying to my partner, Ronnie. Gee, people say Amsterdam is a socialist country, but I cannot use the toilet for free. I have to pay for it if I didn't purchase food at a restaurant. Now, you are in America. Have you ever paid to use a toilet? I don't think so. There are plenty of times, when I am in manhattan and I need to use the toilet. Do you know what I do? I just go to the nearest restaurants and say, hi. where is the bathroom? They point it to me and I use it for free, even though I have never eaten a meal there. That my friend is the difference between a socialist country and a capitalist county. Things are not free in a socialist country. You just assume they are. But they are not.

Back to Jane, my live in American nanny. Jane has never left America. Jane doesn't even hold a US passport. Despite all of this, Jane just assumed that socialist would be a better answer for America. I asked Jane if she thinks social security will be around for her, which she was older than 21 but less than 25 years old at the time. of course, Jane said yes. I laughed. I told Jane she needed to figure out another means for retirement. Social security wouldn't be around for her. I am a very optimistic person. Hence, this is why I am able to do my own business, write a book and have faith that things will work out. But I am also realistic. Social security will not be around for us, especially for those who are under the age of 45 years old. This my friend is an example of a socialist program that is broken. Why would you want to introduce more socialist program to America when we already have a few and they are not working?

MEDICAID

Medicaid is another socialist program. It is run by the government for the public. Have you been reading lately about what is going on with medicaid?[9] When you are on Medicaid, you have poorer access to healthcare.[10] While writing this paragraph, I don't even feel I need to do much research. I think my experience of being poor and just talking to poor people is enough to show me that Medicaid is a broken record and it cannot be fixed. But of course, Medicaid is another example of a socialist program that just doesn't work. I know. I know. I will obtain a lot of hate emails and messages from the democrats die hard fan, who feel this broken record of Medicaid is working. Do you think people really want to be on Medicaid? It is because they either cannot do better, or they are too poor to get something better. But the reality is that medicaid is a horrible, medical program. Articles and researches are showing that people do not get top doctors when they are on medicaid because the reimbursement rate for doctors are so low, that most top doctors won't accept

---

9   http://www.heritage.org/health-care-reform/report/studies-show-medic-aid-patients-have-worse-access-and-outcomes-the
10   http://www.heritage.org/health-care-reform/report/studies-show-medic-aid-patients-have-worse-access-and-outcomes-the

it.[11] Time is what is valuable and I think doctors do not have any shortage of patients. If you could only see 100 patient in a day, and you have 200 knocking down on your door, wouldn't you just take the ones that pay you the full amount? I am not promoting what doctors are doing. But you know, many doctors are leaving medical school with over $200,000 in student loans, courtesy of our broken Government. The only way to pay back for student loan is to charge high fees to the society they (doctors) serve). So how can a doctor take medicaid when they (doctors) have student loans to service? Anyway, this is just another reason socialism doesn't work. In Europe, doctors do not graduate with $200,000 worth of student loans. So when the government in Europe is reimbursing the doctors a small portion of the money owed, those doctors will gladly take it because those doctors in Europe do not have the overheads doctors here in America have. And do not forget the cost of litigation here in America. Doctors get sued like lawsuits are getting out of style. Malpractice insurance cost an arm and a leg. And because of this, why would a doctor take medicaid when malpractice insurance has added to the carrying cost of being in business. Again, this is why socialist work in Europe and not America. America is just a different beast and we in America have tried the socialism aspect and the socialism programs just don't work. So let's stop with this socialist talk. And if you insist upon it, then by all means, move to Europe. And let me know how that is going for you.

WHY PROMOTE SOCIALISM WHEN ALL YOU NEED IS TO LIVE FRUGAL.

I am already 42 years old come May 2018. I am very simple. I have a simple car. I wear simple clothes, though they look stylish. I live in a very affluent neighborhood in South Florida. It is

---

11   http://www.heritage.org/health-care-reform/report/studies-show-medicaid-patients-have-worse-access-and-outcomes-the

called Boca Raton, Florida. I think i am living in one of the most expensive zip codes in Boca Raton. and yet still, I do not keep up with the jones. have you ever tried to live Frugal? I don't care if you are making 400.00 per week, you shouldn't be spending all of that money. You should be saving. If you save for yourself, then you do not need to beg the government anything. If you save for yourself, then you do not need to think the government owe you anything. The government doesn't owe us anything. So I am tired of these democrats telling people they should get free stuff. You do not need free stuff. You need to discipline yourself and live frugal. Here are 5 ways to start living frugal. That way you stop depending on the government for a hand out or stop insisting that America becomes a socialist country.

1. PAY YOURSELF FIRST.

I didn't make this up. Many books on wealth have been written about it. And guess what it works. Don't ask me how. Just try it. If you are taking home after taxes, 400 per week, then put aside 40.00 per week. Then force yourself to live off the rest. You will be surprise just how much you save in this short period of time.

2. IT IS A NEED VERSUS A WANT

Winter is coming up. Do you really need to buy that new winter jacket or those winter boots? What happen to the winter jacket you had last year or the winter boots you had from last year? You need to figure out which one of your impulses are want versus need. If you want it, then you do not have to have it. If you need it, then that is a different story.

3. Cut back on eating out

Have you ever been to a restaurant on Fridays and Saturdays? It is full of people who just got their pay check and what do they do? They blow it on a dinner. Really, can't you just go to the local supermarket and buy yourself a nice piece of steak? Do you know how much money you will save if you cut back on eating out every single weekend? I get it. You need to relax. But this is a bad habit that most Americans form over their life. Cut back. Instead of eating out every weekend. Try every other weekend. And then bring it down to once per month. Trust me. You won't even miss eating out. Besides when you eat out, you are not eating that healthy anyway. I thank God for my kids now. They are 4 years old. And they have no patience when we go out to eat. So this forces me to do a lot of eating at home. My kids are also picky eaters. So it is hard to take them out for food.

4. Cut back on grocery shopping

This seems to be one of the easiest thing to do. Most people asked me to help them with a budget because my friends, client and family know that I am very frugal. They know I live frugal ever single day. I think I told you when I went to college at 19 years old. I didn't have wealthy parents. I had to send myself to school. And I found out from a long time that you can go for days with no food (up to 3 days to be exact). I am not telling you to do that. That is what I did to send myself to college. I was only 19 years old and I was very skinny. By the way the joke about things is that wealthy women and models starve to get those bodies they have. I am not telling you to starve. But you most admit. You look at the average American, he or she could lose some weight. Americans are too overweight and if they cut back on some of that eating they do, they would be healthy for sure and they would save money on their grocery bill. So I feel that a grocery bill, it most of a want versus a need. Okay, so you need to buy bread. Why buy an Italian bread, when you can buy a cheaper bread than that? Because it taste good. Well, your wallet needs a diet? So try to buy a cheaper bread. Do you really need paper towels? When we visited Europe, we noticed very little paper towels. Europeans do not use paper towels. If you go to Jamaica or China, you won't find paper towels either. Do you know you can just use a regular towel. Buy a few at the dollar store and then wash them. That is cheaper and they last longer than paper towels. Protein. Can you look for cheaper protein to eat, like Chicken. I eat chicken around 3 times per week because it is cheap and it taste good. If you have to have beef, why not just do burgers. Those taste good and they are cheap as well. Look at your grocery bill every week and then look how much food you throw out. Then calculate how much food you have been throwing out. Cut the bill by the amount of food you are waisting. They always said do not go to the grocery store hungry or without a list. If you have a list. You will be forced to stick to it.

5. Cut bak on Utility bills.

You can save on light, water, cable and cellular phone. Who is using cable these days? Most of us just watch Netflix or youtube. Take the young generation for instance. Those people hardly watch cable. With the wifi, you can entertain yourself and watch stuff on Netflix or you tube. The average cable bill is $70.00 per month. If you must have cable, then consider dish network. It is cheaper and have a lot of channel. I know, during the football season, most people want cable. Then get the cable for the football season and when the foot ball season is over, cancel the cable or down grade it to basic. You know the time you spend watching television, you could be reading books on how to improve your life. I always believe television is a big waist of time. I am already 42 come May 2018. It means I have less time on this earth. I am going to do things that make me happy and productive. I think you should too. Phone bills. That is the biggie. Shop around. You shouldn't be paying $200.00 per month for a phone bill. If you are paying that much, then you are being ripped off. I am a lawyer and I get many calls. My phone bill on an average basis does not exceed $100.00 per month. And getting the newest and latest phone. Wow. What a rip off that is. Do you really need to spend $300.00 and upwards on the latest phone? What is wrong with the one you have? Just keep the gadget until it is broken. The only exception is of course, your company is paying for it or your job requires it. Aside from that, you are just waisting money.

By becoming frugal, you are providing for yourself and your family and you are not caught up in the government propaganda of socialism and its lack of support for you. By becoming frugal, you will live a lot better than on welfare, as the democratic party would like to lead us to. To live frugality will be a challenge at first. But like any habit, you will get use to it.

Chapter 15

WE HAVE THE RIGHT TO BEAR ARMS AND NO ONE CAN TAKE THIS FROM US.

I was finished writing my book and then Wham. A Horrible thing happened. An evil person shot and killed 58 innocent people in Las Vegas with a gun. This evil man was such a coward that when police came in on him, this evil man ended up killing himself, rather than face justice. My heart breaks for the victims and their families. Sadly, the liberal media and the democrats quickly pounce on this incident and starting making this thing tragedy a gun rights debate. I believe Mrs. Clinton was one of the first to come out swinging that something to this effect: "the NRA (National Rifle Association) is one of the most powerful lobbyist in America. And we must do something about it (NRA)." Bear in mind that Mrs. Clinton is being protected by the secret service, who carry guns. So don't you think this is kind of hypocritical that the very person who is saying that individual shouldn't have gun, is benefitting daily from others who carry guns? Let me explain a few things here. I was in London in September 2017. And people are not afraid of guns there in London. Because many people do not have guns in London. However, there are evil people everywhere. And these evil people do not need guns to terrorize us. There are other evil things out there to harm you. When I was in London, I read the British paper that one guy threw acid on around 5 others in the district of London. That acid injured 5 innocent people.

People I am here to tell you that Guns can kill you. Stress can kill you. Airplanes can kill you. Cars can kill you. People can kill you. Knife can kill you. Cancer can kill you. HIV can kill you. Do you see how silly this sound? Do you think gun is the only thing that can harm a human life? Do you know why the democrats would like to take the gun away from us? It is simple? Power. The United States government wants to have all the power and the United States government wants the people to have no power. So how does the U.S Government take power from the people? It takes the people's gun. I don't need to write an entire chapter on this. People understand that guns give them power. and we need to stop buying into stories that Guns kill people. Because Guns are not the only things to kill people. Stress, diseases, vehicles and people kill people. Here are 4 really sad stories in which Guns did not cause the tragedy.

1. 2016 NICE ATTACK

On July 14, 2017, a large cargo truck's driver, intentionally drove into a crowd in Nice, Franc, killing 86 people and injuring another 458.00. The killer didn't use a gun. The killer used a truck to kill innocent people. I am not making light of the incident. What I am trying to tell people is that look at this awful incident. Guns do kill people. But trucks do as well. 86 people got ruined down. This is horrible. Where are the anti-gun advocates out there? Why aren't they trying to make rules against vehicles? after all this was a tragedy But of course, it didn't involve guns, so no one is really talking. I am trying to show you that evil is what is responsible for death and people can die from other means if there are not guns.

2. HITLER KILLED 6 MILLION INNOCENT JEWISH PEOPLE, AND NOT ALL WITH GUNS

The holocaust is a tragedy and it should never have happened. But do you know that scholars are saying that it might not have happened had the gun control laws not be so tuff. Do you know that many people are saying that Hitler didn't allow the Jewish to own guns? Let me Just say something. I am not making light of the holocaust. My two nieces are half jewish. My brother in Law David DeSouza father's was the Rabbi in Jamaica, the West Indies. The name of the Synagogue in Jamaica is Shaare Shalom Synagogue, of Kingston, Jamaica if anyone care to look it up. I believe that Hitler did the work of the devil. The holocaust is pure evil and it will always be reflected in people's mind as of the most evil things to have ever been done on planet earth. I am just saying that I along with other scholars believed that Hitler got the upper hands on one group of population because that group was not able to get their hands on guns.   And because of that, the jewish people became too vulnerable to a revolution. Also, do you noticed that even though 6 Million jewish died during the holocaust, most didn't die from a gunshot? No Hitler and his people took them to concentration camp and starve these innocent jewish people. I am not making light of anything. and I am not a racist. My brother in law is jewish and I have dated a jewish man before. I am planning on going to Israel in 2020 because as a christian, Israel is near and dear to us. On my vacation to Amsterdam, I visited the Ann Franks museum. I love the jewish population and I have no intention of making light of the jewish tragedy that took place by the Nazi. I am just trying to show you that many people are puzzled as to why the jewish population didn't fight back against Hitler and the Nazis? Well, one of those answers are the fact that the jewish people were not allowed to own guns. .But I can just imagine a tyrant like Adolph Hitler use the advantage of one population not being able to arm themselves, as a way to kill them (the Jews).[12] We can not let history repeat itself. There is no way the government should tell us we cannot bear arms. This is a deadly situation where the government can someone over throw us in our own homes. Do not let the government take the power from you. You have a right to bear arms. And you have a right to defend yourself in the comfort of your home. You must bear arms. That is the basic core of being human.

3. SEPTEMBER 11, 2001 ATTACK

Now, you know that September 11, attack in America was one of the worst attack we had on human soil. This killed many people and we cannot underestimate the power of terrorist. But it is obvious that Guns were not to be blamed for the attacks. These evil people were a bunch of terrorists that used airplanes as weapons to terrorized and killed many Americans.

Here are 3 examples of when a Gun was used to benefit another person.

71 YEAR OLD WOMAN SHOT AN INTRODUCER

It was reported that in 2001, a 71 year old invalid shot and wounded a person who broke into her house and knocked her down to the floor. God only knows if the 71 year old would be alive today had it not been for her quick acting and the gun she carried.[13]

---

12   https://en.wikipedia.org/wiki/Nazi_gun_control_theory
13   https://www.gunowners.org/sk0205.htm

83 YEAR OLD WOMAN SHOT A TEENAGER

It was reported that a 83 year old woman shot a teenager as the teenager tried to rob her (the 83 year old). Again, only God knows if this 83 year old would have been alive had it not been the quick thinking and the defense of a gun being used. You cannot assume that someone who is breaking into your home is going to mean you any good. And so if you break into someone home, you probably deserve to be shot.[14]

2 ROBBERS POINTED A SEMIAUTOMATIC GUN WEAPONS AT OWNER

In Pembroke Pines, Florida, two armed robbers entered a store and pointed their semiautomatic guns at the owner. Luckily the store owner was armed. The store owner ended up taking out his own gun and shooting both of these armed robberies. Do not tell me you think the news would have ended up any other way had the owner not been armed. Do you think these robberies were going into the store with their semi-automatic guns just to have a nice conversation with the owner? or do you think these thugs would be afraid to use their weapon? Let's not pretend the world isn't full of evil and people need to defend themselves against evil all the time.[15]

I hope this books has open your eyes and your mind to the good of the Republican party and President Trump. Even though I must sign off now, It it not good bye forever. Please drop me a line. You can find my email anywhere on the internet. But just in case, I can be reached directly at tlaw45@hotmail.com If I ever do a book tour on this book, or any book that I go on to write, then please stop by to say hello. I promised to chat with you and

14   https://www.gunowners.org/sk0205.htm
15   https://www.gunowners.org/sk0205.htm

sign a book or two. If you hear me on my radio program, then call in. I would love to hear from you. Until next time, good bye and God bless you and your family. God bless America. God Bless the Republican Party. God bless President Donald J. Trump.

CREDITS FOR CHAPTER 11 BIOGRAPHY

16

DNC[17]

Trump?[18]

information,[19]

---

16   United States intelligence agencies have concluded that there was Russian interference in the 2016 United States elections.[1][2][3] In January 2017, a published U.S. intelligence community assessment expressed "high confidence" that the Russian government favored Donald Trump over Hillary Clinton and that Russian President Vladimir Putin personally ordered an "influence campaign" to denigrate Clinton and to harm her electoral chances and potential presidency.[4] The report concluded that Russia used disinformation, data thefts, leaks, and social media "trolls" in an effort to give an advantage to Trump over Clinton but did not target or compromise vote tallying. https://en.wikipedia.org/wiki/Russian_interference_in_the_2016_United_States_elections

17   On October 7, 2016,[7] the Office of the Director of National Intelligence (DNI) and the Department of Homeland Security (DHS) jointly stated that Russia hacked the Democratic National Committee (DNC) servers and Clinton campaign chairman John Podesta's personal email account and leaked their documents to WikiLeaks.[8][9] Several cybersecurity firms stated that the cyberattacks were committed by Russian intelligence groups Fancy Bear and Cozy Bear   https://en.wikipedia.org/wiki/Russian_interference_in_the_2016_United_States_elections

18   The report concluded that Russia used disinformation, data thefts, leaks, and social media "trolls" in an effort to give an advantage to Trump over Clinton but did not target or compromise vote tallying.[1] These conclusions were reaffirmed by the lead intelligence officials in the Trump administration in May 2017.[5] Intelligence allies of the U.S. in Europe had found communications between suspected Russian agents and the Trump campaign as early as 2015.[https://en.wikipedia.org/wiki/Russian_interference_in_the_2016_United_States_elections

19   We can speculate, though, on what the Russians could have done after they gained access to the election officials' computers. For example, they could have deleted records for voters registered with one party to help candidates of the other party. Deleted voters would have still been able to vote, but they would have had to cast provisional ballots — a cumbersome process that could have discouraged some from casting their votes. Attackers could also have simply caused registration systems to crash in precincts that were likely to vote heavily for one candidate over the other. That could

vote.[20]

hacking.[21]

hackers.[22]

over.[23]

---

have caused delays and long lines that would suppress turnout in those precincts. https://www.vox.com/new-money/2017/6/6/15745888/russia-election-hacking-leak

20 Russia's GRU intelligence agency attempted to hack the computers of voting officials across the country in the days before the 2016 presidential election, according to a top secret National Security Agency document that was leaked to the Intercept.

The attacks focused on voter registration systems rather than voting machines themselves, so there's no evidence that the Russian government directly changed anyone's vote. But there's also a lot we can't tell from the report about what the Russians might have accomplished — and whether they could have altered the election result, directly or indirectly.

We can speculate, though, on what the Russians could have done after they gained access to the election officials' computers. For example, they could have deleted records for voters registered with one party to help candidates of the other party. Deleted voters would have still been able to vote, but they would have had to cast provisional ballots — a cumbersome process that could have discouraged some from casting their votes. https://www.vox.com/new-money/2017/6/6/15745888/russia-election-hacking-leak

21 At least one jurisdiction using EV Systems voting technology experienced serious glitches on election day: Durham, North Carolina. The voter registration system there malfunctioned, leading to long lines. Officials there say they don't believe they were hacked — they say the problems they encountered appeared to be the result of user error. But Alex Halderman, a computer security expert at the University of Michigan, points out that if a sophisticated hacker were targeting American elections, it would do what it could to make any glitches appear to be accidents rather than deliberate sabotage https://www.vox.com/new-money/2017/6/6/15745888/russia-election-hacking-leak

22 But Alex Halderman, a computer security expert at the University of Michigan, points out that if a sophisticated hacker were targeting American elections, it would do what it could to make any glitches appear to be accidents rather than deliberate sabotage. https://www.vox.com/new-money/2017/6/6/15745888/russia-election-hacking-leak

23 Experts on political misinformation see things differently. They worry that the unfounded speculation and paranoia that infect the Russiasphere risk pushing liberals into the same black hole of conspiracy-mongering and fact-free insinuation that conservatives fell into during the Obama years.

power.[24] Russians.[25]
Kremlins.[26] government.[27].

The fear is that this pollutes the party itself, derailing and discrediting the legitimate investigation into Russia investigation. It also risks degrading the Democratic Party — helping elevate shameless hucksters who know nothing about policy but are willing to spread misinformation in the service of gaining power. We've already seen this story play out on the right, a story that ended in Trump's election.

"One of the failures of the Republican Party is the way they let the birther movement metastasize — and that ultimately helped Donald Trump make it to the White House," says Brendan Nyhan, a professor at Dartmouth who studies the spread of false political beliefs. https://www.vox.com/world/2017/5/19/15561842/trump-russia-louise-mensch

24   President Donald Trump is about to resign as a result of the Russia scandal. Bernie Sanders and Sean Hannity are Russian agents. The Russians have paid off House Oversight Chair Jason Chaffetz to the tune of $10 million, using Trump as a go-between. Paul Ryan is a traitor for refusing to investigate Trump's Russia ties. Libertarian heroine Ayn Rand was a secret Russian agent charged with discrediting the American conservative movement.

These are all claims you can find made on a new and growing sector of the internet that functions as a fake news bubble for liberals, something I've dubbed the Russiasphere. The mirror image of Breitbart and InfoWars on the right, it focuses nearly exclusively on real and imagined connections between Trump and Russia. The tone is breathless: full of unnamed intelligence sources, certainty that Trump will soon be imprisoned, and fever dream factual assertions that no reputable media outlet has managed to confirm. https://www.vox.com/world/2017/5/19/15561842/trump-russia-louise-mensch

25   There's also a handful of websites, like Palmer Report, that seem devoted nearly exclusively to spreading bizarre assertions like the theory that Ryan and Sen. Majority Leader Mitch McConnell funneled Russian money to Trump — a story that spread widely among the site's 70,000 Facebook fans https://www.vox.com/world/2017/5/19/15561842/trump-russia-louise-mensch

26   On Friday, The Washington Post broke a bombshell report that President Trump's senior adviser and son-in-law Jared Kushner proposed setting up a back-channel of communication between Trump and Moscow using Russian facilities.
Over the next two days, the president's staff took to the airwaves to downplay concerns about the gravity of the situation http://www.businessinsider.com/trump-kushner-russia-backchannel-ties-2017-5

27   On Saturday, national security adviser H.R. McMaster told reporters that he "would not be concerned about a back-channel" between Trump and the Kremlin.
"We have back-channel communications with a number of countries. So, generally speaking, about back-channel communications, what that allows you to do is to com-

do."[28]

piece.[29] it.[30]

," a election?[31] DNC[32] Trump?[33]

---

municate in a discreet manner," McMaster said.
On Sunday, Department of Homeland Security secretary John Kelly told NBC's Chuck Todd that he was not bothered by the revelations either.

Kushner's "number one interest, really, is the nation. So you know there's a lot of different ways to communicate, back-channel, publicly with other countries," Kelly said. "I don't see any big issue here relative to Jared." http://www.businessinsider.com/trump-kushner-russia-backchannel-ties-2017-5

28   http://www.cnn.com/2017/06/29/opinions/much-ado-about-nothing-burger-van-jones/index.html

29   http://www.cnn.com/2017/06/29/opinions/much-ado-about-nothing-burger-van-jones/index.html

30   I am glad there is a Russia investigation, and I hope they get to the bottom of it. But I think Democrats are fooling ourselves if we think that something is going to come out of this investigation that is somehow going to end the Trump presidency and make everything better. Unless there is a real smoking gun, which there is probably not, it's just going to be a big old mess.http://www.cnn.com/2017/06/29/opinions/much-ado-about-nothing-burger-van-jones/index.html

31   United States intelligence agencies have concluded that there was Russian interference in the 2016 United States elections.[1][2][3] In January 2017, a published U.S. intelligence community assessment expressed "high confidence" that the Russian government favored Donald Trump over Hillary Clinton and that Russian President Vladimir Putin personally ordered an "influence campaign" to denigrate Clinton and to harm her electoral chances and potential presidency.[4] The report concluded that Russia used disinformation, data thefts, leaks, and social media "trolls" in an effort to give an advantage to Trump over Clinton but did not target or compromise vote tallying. https://en.wikipedia.org/wiki/Russian_interference_in_the_2016_United_States_elections

32   On October 7, 2016,[7] the Office of the Director of National Intelligence (DNI) and the Department of Homeland Security (DHS) jointly stated that Russia hacked the Democratic National Committee (DNC) servers and Clinton campaign chairman John Podesta's personal email account and leaked their documents to WikiLeaks.[8][9] Several cybersecurity firms stated that the cyberattacks were committed by Russian intelligence groups Fancy Bear and Cozy Bear https://en.wikipedia.org/wiki/Russian_interference_in_the_2016_United_States_elections

33   The report concluded that Russia used disinformation, data thefts, leaks, and social media "trolls" in an effort to give an advantage to Trump over Clinton but did

information,[34] vote.[35] hacking.[36] hackers.[37]

not target or compromise vote tallying.[1] These conclusions were reaffirmed by the lead intelligence officials in the Trump administration in May 2017.[5] Intelligence allies of the U.S. in Europe had found communications between suspected Russian agents and the Trump campaign as early as 2015. [https://en.wikipedia.org/wiki/Russian interference in the 2016 United States elections

34   We can speculate, though, on what the Russians could have done after they gained access to the election officials' computers. For example, they could have deleted records for voters registered with one party to help candidates of the other party. Deleted voters would have still been able to vote, but they would have had to cast provisional ballots — a cumbersome process that could have discouraged some from casting their votes.

Attackers could also have simply caused registration systems to crash in precincts that were likely to vote heavily for one candidate over the other. That could have caused delays and long lines that would suppress turnout in those precincts. https://www.vox.com/new-money/2017/6/6/15745888/russia-election-hacking-leak

35   Russia's GRU intelligence agency attempted to hack the computers of voting officials across the country in the days before the 2016 presidential election, according to a top secret National Security Agency document that was leaked to the Intercept.

The attacks focused on voter registration systems rather than voting machines themselves, so there's no evidence that the Russian government directly changed anyone's vote. But there's also a lot we can't tell from the report about what the Russians might have accomplished — and whether they could have altered the election result, directly or indirectly.

We can speculate, though, on what the Russians could have done after they gained access to the election officials' computers. For example, they could have deleted records for voters registered with one party to help candidates of the other party. Deleted voters would have still been able to vote, but they would have had to cast provisional ballots — a cumbersome process that could have discouraged some from casting their votes. https://www.vox.com/new-money/2017/6/6/15745888/russia-election-hacking-leak

36   At least one jurisdiction using EV Systems voting technology experienced serious glitches on election day: Durham, North Carolina. The voter registration system there malfunctioned, leading to long lines. Officials there say they don't believe they were hacked — they say the problems they encountered appeared to be the result of user error. But Alex Halderman, a computer security expert at the University of Michigan, points out that if a sophisticated hacker were targeting American elections, it would do what it could to make any glitches appear to be accidents rather than deliberate sabotage https://www.vox.com/new-money/2017/6/6/15745888/russia-election-hacking-leak

37   But Alex Halderman, a computer security expert at the University of Mich-

hacked[38]   over.[39]

---

igan, points out that if a sophisticated hacker were targeting American elections, it would do what it could to make any glitches appear to be accidents rather than deliberate sabotage. https://www.vox.com/new-money/2017/6/6/15745888/russia-election-hacking-leak

38   In the run-up to the election, the US Democratic National Committee (DNC) received numerous phishing emails, the paper reported on Tuesday. One of them was also sent to John Podesta, the chairman of Hillary Clinton's campaign. An aide, Charles Delavan, spotted the message sent to Podesta's private account. It asked Podesta to change his password. Delavan realised the email was a phishing attack and forwarded it to a computer technician. However, he made a typo, writing: "This is a legitimate email." He added: "John needs to change his password immediately." https://www.theguardian.com/us-news/2016/dec/14/dnc-hillary-clinton-emails-hacked-russia-aide-typo-investigation-finds

39   Experts on political misinformation see things differently. They worry that the unfounded speculation and paranoia that infect the Russiasphere risk pushing liberals into the same black hole of conspiracy-mongering and fact-free insinuation that conservatives fell into during the Obama years.

The fear is that this pollutes the party itself, derailing and discrediting the legitimate investigation into Russia investigation. It also risks degrading the Democratic Party — helping elevate shameless hucksters who know nothing about policy but are willing to spread misinformation in the service of gaining power. We've already seen this story play out on the right, a story that ended in Trump's election.

"One of the failures of the Republican Party is the way they let the birther movement metastasize — and that ultimately helped Donald Trump make it to the White House," says Brendan Nyhan, a professor at Dartmouth who studies the spread of false political beliefs. https://www.vox.com/world/2017/5/19/15561842/trump-russia-louise-mensch

power.[40] Russians.[41]

---

40   President Donald Trump is about to resign as a result of the Russia scandal. Bernie Sanders and Sean Hannity are Russian agents. The Russians have paid off House Oversight Chair Jason Chaffetz to the tune of $10 million, using Trump as a go-between. Paul Ryan is a traitor for refusing to investigate Trump's Russia ties. Libertarian heroine Ayn Rand was a secret Russian agent charged with discrediting the American conservative movement.

These are all claims you can find made on a new and growing sector of the internet that functions as a fake news bubble for liberals, something I've dubbed the Russiasphere. The mirror image of Breitbart and InfoWars on the right, it focuses nearly exclusively on real and imagined connections between Trump and Russia. The tone is breathless: full of unnamed intelligence sources, certainty that Trump will soon be imprisoned, and fever dream factual assertions that no reputable media outlet has managed to confirm. https://www.vox.com/world/2017/5/19/15561842/trump-russia-louise-mensch

41   There's also a handful of websites, like Palmer Report, that seem devoted nearly exclusively to spreading bizarre assertions like the theory that Ryan and Sen. Majority Leader Mitch McConnell funneled Russian money to Trump — a story that spread widely among the site's 70,000 Facebook fans https://www.vox.com/world/2017/5/19/15561842/trump-russia-louise-mensch

Kremlins.[42] government.[43] corruption.[44]
do."[45]
piece.[46] it.[47]

---

42   On Friday, The Washington Post broke a bombshell report that President Trump's senior adviser and son-in-law Jared Kushner proposed setting up a back-channel of communication between Trump and Moscow using Russian facilities.
Over the next two days, the president's staff took to the airwaves to downplay concerns about the gravity of the situation http://www.businessinsider.com/trump-kushner-russia-backchannel-ties-2017-5

43   On Saturday, national security adviser H.R. McMaster told reporters that he "would not be concerned about a back-channel" between Trump and the Kremlin.

"We have back-channel communications with a number of countries. So, generally speaking, about back-channel communications, what that allows you to do is to communicate in a discreet manner," McMaster said.

On Sunday, Department of Homeland Security secretary John Kelly told NBC's Chuck Todd that he was not bothered by the revelations either.

Kushner's "number one interest, really, is the nation. So you know there's a lot of different ways to communicate, back-channel, publicly with other countries," Kelly said. "I don't see any big issue here relative to Jared." http://www.businessinsider.com/trump-kushner-russia-backchannel-ties-2017-5

44   "The idea of using Russian facilities to skirt Russian surveillance in the US would either be a serious attempt to hide something or the actions of a young amateur," Clint Watts, a former FBI agent and fellow at the Foreign Policy Research Institute, told The Atlantic. http://www.businessinsider.com/trump-kushner-russia-back-channel-ties-2017-5

45   http://www.cnn.com/2017/06/29/opinions/much-ado-about-nothing-burger-van-jones/index.html

46   http://www.cnn.com/2017/06/29/opinions/much-ado-about-nothing-burger-van-jones/index.html

47   I am glad there is a Russia investigation, and I hope they get to the bottom of it. But I think Democrats are fooling ourselves if we think that something is going to come out of this investigation that is somehow going to end the Trump presidency and make everything better. Unless there is a real smoking gun, which there is probably not, it's just going to be a big old mess. http://www.cnn.com/2017/06/29/opinions/much-ado-about-nothing-burger-van-jones/index.html

About The Author

Teisha Powell is a licensed attorney in the State of Florida and an author, radio and television personality. A highly sought out political pundit, Ms. Powell is a regular guest on national cable television shows discussing and debating political issues on national TV, which includes FOX, RT, ITV24, and NEWSMAX to name a few. Ms. Powell has worked on many national campaigns mostly notable republicans including 2008 John McCain for President. Ms Powell's law practice in the State of Florida focuses primarily on insurance claims, personal injury claims and slip and fall claims. Ms. Powell is available for speaking and media appearances. For more information on Ms. Powell, please visit her web page at www.insurancelawyertish.com or email lawyerpowell@gmail.com; https://www.facebook.com/TeishaPowellFL/ Or Twitter @teisha_powell